COLORADO TRAILS

SOUTH-CENTRAL REGION

Warning: While every effort has been made to make the trail descriptions in this book as accurate as possible, some discrepancies may exist between the text and the actual trail. Hazards may have changed since the research and publication of this edition. Adler Publishing Company, Inc., and the authors accept no responsibility for the safety of users of this guide. Individuals are liable for all costs incurred if rescue is necessary.

Printed in the United States of America.

Cover photos
Clockwise from bottom left: Allie Belle Mine Building on Hancock Pass Trail, Medano Pass and Great Sand Dunes Trail, Baldwin Lakes

Rear cover photos
From left: Fishing at Mirror Lake on Tincup Pass Trail, Alpine Station on Alpine Tunnel Trail

COLORADO TRAILS
SOUTH-CENTRAL REGION

PETER MASSEY
JEANNE WILSON

ADLER
PUBLISHING

Acknowledgements

We would like to express gratitude to the staff at the U.S. Forest Service, the Denver Public Library, the Colorado Historical Society, and the various Chambers of Commerce throughout Colorado who have given us guidance in our research.

We would like to recognize especially the following for their major contributions to this endeavor:

Cover Design Concept: **Rudy Ramos**
Text Design and Maps: **Deborah Rust Design**
Copyediting: **Alice Levine**
Proofreading: **James Barnett**

Contents

Using This Book

Route Planning

The regional map on page 16 provides an overview of the trails in this book. Each 4WD trail is highlighted, as are major highways and towns, which makes it possible to relate the start and end points of every 4WD trail in this book to nearby roads and trails.

By referring to the map you can plan your overall route to utilize as many 4WD trails as possible. Checking the difficulty rating and time required for each trail allows you to finalize your plans.

Difficulty Ratings

We utilize a point system to indicate the difficulty of each trail. Any such system is subjective and is dependent on the driver's experience level and the current road conditions.

We have rated the 4WD trails in this book on a scale of 1 to 10, 1 being passable for a normal passenger vehicle in good conditions and 10 requiring a heavily modified vehicle and an experienced driver who is willing to expect vehicle damage. Because this book is designed for owners of unmodified 4WD vehicles whom we assume do not want to risk damage to their vehicles, nearly all the trails are rated 5 or lower.

This is not to say that all the trails in this book are easy. We strongly recommend that inexperienced drivers not tackle any 4- or 5-rated trails before undertaking a number of the lower-rated ones, so that they can gauge their skill level and prepare for the difficulty of the higher-rated trails.

In assessing the trails, we assume good road conditions (dry road surface, good visibility, and so on). Our ratings are based on the following factors:

■ obstacles such as rocks, mud, ruts, and stream crossings
■ the stability of the road surface
■ the width of the road and the vehicle clearance between trees or rocks
■ the steepness of the road
■ the margin of error (for example, a very high, open shelf road would be rated more difficult even if it was not very steep and had a stable surface)

The following is a guide to the ratings. As a rule only one of the criteria need to be met for the road to get a higher rating:

Rating 1: Graded dirt but suitable for a normal passenger vehicle. Gentle grades; fairly wide; very shallow water crossings (if any).

Rating 2: Road surface rarely or not maintained. Dirt road better suited to a high-clearance vehicle but passable in a normal passenger car; fairly wide, passing not a concern; mud not a concern under normal weather conditions.

Rating 3: High-clearance 4WD preferred. Rough road surface to be expected; mud possible but easily passable; rocks up to six inches in diameter; loose surface possible; shelf road but wide enough for passing or with adequate pull-offs.

Rating 4: High-clearance 4WD recommended. Rough road surface with rocks larger than six inches possible, but a reasonable driving line available; mud possible but passable; stream crossings less than fifteen inches deep; substantial sections of single-lane shelf road possible; moderate grades; moderately loose surface possible.

Rating 5: High-clearance 4WD required. Rough, rutted surface; rocks up to nine inches possible; mud may be impassable for inexperienced drivers; stream crossings up to twenty-four inches deep; sections may be steep enough to cause traction problems; very narrow shelf road with steep drop-offs should be expected; tight clearance between rocks or trees possible.

Rating 6: Experienced four-wheel drivers only. Potentially dangerous; large rocks, ruts, or terraces may need to be negotiated; steep slopes, loose surface, and/or very narrow vehicle clearance; stream crossings at least twenty-four inches deep, and/or unstable stream bottom, or difficult access; very narrow shelf road with steep drop-offs and challenging road surfaces to be expected.

Rating 7: Skilled, experienced four-wheel drivers only. Very challenging sections; very steep sections likely; loose surface, large rocks, deep ruts, and tight clearance expected; mud likely to necessitate winching.

Rating 8 to 10: Stock vehicles are likely to be damaged and may find the trail impassable. Well beyond the scope of this book.

Scenic Ratings

If rating the degree of difficulty is subjective, rating scenic beauty is guaranteed to lead to arguments—especially in Colorado, a stunningly beautiful state. However, we have tried to give some guide to the relative scenic quality of the various trails. The ratings are based on a scale of 1 to 10, with 10 being the most scenic.

Estimated Driving Times

In calculating driving times, we have not allowed for stops. Actual driving time may be considerably longer than indicated, depending on the number and duration of stops. Add more time if you prefer to drive more slowly than good conditions allow.

As with the distance cited for each trail, the time given for trails that dead-end is for travel one-way. The time that should be allowed for the overall trip, including the return to the start, may be as much as dou-

ble that indicated. However, with the knowledge of the trail that has been gained going in, you may find that the return is usually completed more quickly.

Current Road Conditions

All the 4WD trails described in this book may be impassable in poor weather conditions. For each trail, we have provided a phone number for obtaining current information about conditions.

Abbreviations

The route directions provided for the 4WD trails in this book use a series of abbreviations.

SO	Continue straight on
TL	Turn left
TR	Turn right
BL	Bear left
BR	Bear right
UT	U-turn

Using Route Directions

To help you stay on track, we have described and pinpointed (by odometer reading) nearly every significant feature along the route (intersections, streams, gates, cattle guards, and so on) and have provided directions to follow from these landmarks. Odometer readings will vary from vehicle to vehicle, but you will soon learn to allow for slight variations.

If you diverge from the route, zero your trip meter upon your return and continue the route, making the necessary adjustment to the point-to-point odometer directions. We have regularly reset the odometer readings in the directions, so you won't have to recalculate for too long. Route directions include cross-references whenever the route crosses another 4WD trail included in this book, which allows easy change of route or destination. Directions for traveling the 4WD trails in reverse are printed in green. When traveling in reverse, read from the bottom of the table and work up.

Latitude and longitude readings are provided periodically to facilitate the use of a

Global Positioning System (GPS) receiver. These readings may also assist in finding your location on your maps. The GPS coordinates were taken using the NAD 1927 datum and are in the format dd°mm.mmm'. When loading coordinates into your GPS receiver, you may wish to include only one decimal place because in Colorado, the third decimal place equals only about two yards and the second less than twenty yards.

Map References

We recommend that you supplement the information in this book with more-detailed maps. Each trail in this book refers to various sheet maps and road atlases that provide the detail necessary to navigate and identify accurately your location. Typically, the following five references are given:

■ U.S. Forest Service Maps—Scale 1:126,720

■ U.S. Geological Survey County Series Maps—Scale 1:50,000

■ *The Roads of Colorado*, 1st ed. (Fredericksburg, Texas: Shearer Publishing, 1996)—Scale 1:158,400

■ *Colorado Atlas & Gazetteer*, 2nd ed. (Freeport, Maine: DeLorme Mapping, 1995)—Scale 1:160,000 and 1:320,000

■ *Trails Illustrated* topo maps; National Geographic maps—Various scales, but all contain good detail

We recommend the *Trails Illustrated* maps. They are reliable, easy to read, and printed on nearly indestructible plastic "paper." However, the series does not cover all the 4WD trails described in this book.

If *Trails Illustrated* maps are not available, we recommend the U.S. Geological Survey County Series Maps. These show the necessary detail without being too detailed. Their main weakness is that some are out of date and do not show the 4WD trails accurately.

The two atlases are reasonably priced and include maps of the entire state. Although the atlases do not give much information for each 4WD trail beyond what we have provided, they are helpful if you wish to explore side roads. Of the two,

we prefer *The Roads of Colorado.*

U.S. Forest Service maps lack the detail of the other sheet maps and, in our experience, are also out of date occasionally. They have the advantage of covering a broad area. These maps are most useful for the longer trails.

For those who want to navigate with the assistance of a portable computer, Maptech publishes a particularly good series of maps on CD ROM. These are based on the U.S. Geological Survey 7.5° Series Maps—Scale 1:24,000, but they can be viewed on four scales. The 1:100,000-scale series are also included. These maps offer many advantages over normal maps:

■ GPS coordinates for any location can be found, which can then be loaded into your GPS receiver. Conversely, if you know your GPS coordinates, your location on the map can be pinpointed instantly.

■ Towns, rivers, passes, mountains, and many other sites are indexed by name so that they can be located quickly.

■ 4WD trails can be marked and profiled for elevation change and distance from point to point.

■ Customized maps can be printed out.

To cover the entire state of Colorado requires 8 CD ROMs, which is expensive; however, the CD ROMs can be purchased individually.

All these maps should be available through good map stores. The CD ROMs are available directly from Maptech (800-627-7236 or on the Internet at www.maptech.com).

Driving Off-Highway

Four-wheel driving involves special road rules and techniques. This section is provided as an introduction for 4WD beginners.

4WD Road Rules

To help ensure that these trails remain open and available for all four-wheel drivers to enjoy, it is important to minimize your impact on the environment and not be a safety risk to yourself or anyone else. Remember that the 4WD clubs in Colorado fight a constant battle with the U.S. Forest Service to retain access.

The fundamental rule when traversing the 4WD trails described in this book is to use common sense. In addition, special road rules for 4WD trails apply.

■ Vehicles traveling uphill have the right of way.

■ If you are moving more slowly than the vehicle behind you, pull over to let the other vehicle by.

■ Park out of the way in a safe place. Set the parking brake—don't rely on leaving the transmission in park. Manual transmissions should be left in the lowest gear.

In addition to these rules, we offer the following advice to four-wheel drivers.

■ Size up the situation in advance.

■ Be careful. Take your time.

■ Maintain smooth, steady power and momentum.

■ Engage 4WD and low-range before you get into a tight situation.

■ Steer toward high spots and try to put the wheel over large rocks.

■ Straddle ruts.

■ Use gears rather than only the brakes to hold the vehicle when driving downhill. On very steep slopes, chock the wheels when you park your vehicle.

■ Watch for logging and mining trucks.

■ Wear your seat belt and ensure that all luggage, especially heavy items such as tool boxes or coolers, is secured. Heavy items should be secured by ratchet tie-down straps rather than elastic-type straps, which are not strong enough to hold heavy items if the vehicle rolls.

Tread Lightly!

Remember the rules of the Tread Lightly!® program.

■ Become informed. Obtain maps, regulations, and other information from the U.S. Forest Service or from other public land agencies. Learn the rules and follow them.

■ Resist the urge to pioneer a new road or trail or to cut across a switchback. Stay on constructed tracks and avoid running over young trees, shrubs, and grasses, damaging or killing them. Don't drive across alpine tundra; this fragile environment may take years to recover.

■ Stay off soft, wet roads and 4WD trails readily torn up by vehicles. Repairing the damage is expensive.

■ Travel around meadows, steep hillsides, stream banks, and lake shores that are easily scarred by churning wheels.

■ Stay away from wild animals that are rearing young or suffering from a food shortage.

■ Obey gate closures and regulatory signs.

■ Preserve America's heritage by not disturbing old mining camps, ghost towns, or other historical features.

■ Carry out all rubbish.

■ Stay out of designated wilderness areas. They are closed to all vehicles. Know where the boundaries are.

■ Get permission to cross private land. Leave livestock alone. Respect landowners' rights.

Special Four-Wheel Driving Techniques

Certain obstacles are likely to be encountered on Colorado's 4WD trails. The following provides an introduction to the techniques required for dealing with the most common situations.

Rocks. Tire selection is important because sharp rocks are often encountered on Colorado mountain 4WD trails. Select a multiple-ply, tough sidewall, light-truck tire with a large-lug tread.

As you approach a rocky stretch, get into 4WD low range to give you maximum slow-speed control. Speed is rarely necessary since traction on a rocky surface is usually good. Plan ahead and select the line you wish to take. If the rock appears to be larger than the clearance of your vehicle, don't try to straddle it. Check to see that it is not higher than the frame of your vehicle once you get a wheel over it. Put a wheel up to the rock and slowly climb it; then gently drop over the other side, using the brake to ensure a smooth landing. Bouncing the car over rocks increases the likelihood of damage, as the body's clearance is reduced by the suspension compressing. Running boards also significantly reduce your clearance in this respect.

Steep Uphill Grades. Consider walking the trail to ensure that it is passable, especially if it is clear that backtracking is going to be a problem.

Select 4WD low range to ensure that you have adequate power to pull up the hill. If the wheels begin to lose traction, try turning the steering wheel gently from side to side to give the wheels a chance to regain traction.

If you lose momentum, but the car is not in danger of sliding, use the foot brake, switch off the ignition, leave the vehicle in gear (if manual transmission) or park (if automatic), engage the parking brake, and get out to examine the situation. See if you can remove any obstacles, and figure out the line you need to take. Reversing a couple of yards and starting again may allow you to get better traction and momentum.

If you decide a stretch of road is impassably steep, back down the trail. Trying to turn the vehicle around is extremely dangerous and very likely to cause it to roll over.

Steep Downhill Grades. Again, consider walking the trail to ensure that it is passable, especially if it is clear that backtracking is going to be a problem.

Select 4WD low range, in first gear, to maximize braking assistance from the engine. If the surface is loose and you are losing traction, change up to second or third gear. Do not use the brakes if you can avoid it, but don't let the vehicle's speed get out of control. Feather (lightly pump) the brakes if you slip under braking.

Travel very slowly over rock ledges or ruts. Attempt to tackle these diagonally, letting one wheel down at a time.

If the vehicle begins to slide around at the back, gently apply the throttle and correct the steering. If the rear of the vehicle starts to slide sideways, do not apply the brakes.

Mud. Muddy trails are easily damaged, so they should be avoided if possible. If you do need to traverse a section of mud, your success will depend heavily on whether you have open-lugged mud tires or chains. Thick mud fills the tighter tread that is on normal tires, leaving the tire with no more grip than if it were bald. If the muddy stretch is only a few yards long, the momentum of your vehicle may allow you to get through regardless.

If the muddy track is very steep, either uphill or downhill, do not attempt it. Your vehicle is very likely to skid in such conditions and the vehicle may roll or slip off the edge of the road.

When crossing mud:

■ Avoid making detours off existing tracks, so that environmental damage is minimized.

■ Check to see that the mud has a reasonably firm base (tackling deep mud is definitely not recommended unless you have a vehicle-mounted winch—and even then, be cautious because the winch may not get you out).

■ Check to see that no ruts are too deep for the ground clearance of your vehicle.

Having decided that you can get through and having selected the best route, use the following techniques:

■ Select 4WD low range and a suitable gear; momentum is the key to success, so use a high enough gear to build up sufficient speed.

■ Avoid accelerating heavily, so as to minimize wheel spinning and provide maximum traction.

■ Follow existing wheel ruts, unless they are too deep for the clearance of your vehicle.

■ Correct slides by turning the steering wheel in the direction that the rear wheels are skidding, but don't be too aggressive with the amount you correct your steering.

■ If the vehicle comes to a stop, don't continue to accelerate, as you will only spin your wheels and dig yourself into a rut. Try backing out and having another go.

Stream Crossings. By crossing a stream that is too deep, drivers risk far more than water flowing in and ruining the interior of their vehicles. Water sucked into the engine's air intake will seriously damage the engine. Likewise, water that seeps into the air vent on the transmission or differential will mix with the lubricant and may lead to serious problems. Water that gets into the interior of modern vehicles may damage the computerized vehicle management system. Even worse than damage to a vehicle is the possibility that deep or fast flowing water could easily carry a vehicle downstream and may endanger the lives of the occupants.

The manual for some 4WDs will say what fording depth the vehicle can negotiate safely. If your vehicle's owner's manual doesn't include this information, your local dealer may be able to assist. If you don't know, then you should try to avoid crossing through water that is more than a foot or so deep.

The first rule for crossing a stream is to know what you are getting into. You need to ascertain how deep the water is, make sure that there are no large rocks or holes and that the bottom is solid enough to avoid getting the vehicle bogged, and see that the entry and exit points are negotiable. This assessment may take some time and you may get wet, but to cross a stream without first properly evaluating the situation is to take a great risk.

The secret to water crossings is to keep moving, but not to move too quickly. In shallow water (where the surface of the water is below the bumper), your primary concern is to safely negotiate the bottom of the stream, avoiding any rock damage and maintaining momentum if there is a danger of getting stuck or slipping on the exit.

In deeper water (between eighteen and thirty inches deep), the objective is to create a small bow wave in front of the moving vehicle. This requires a speed that is approximately walking pace. The bow wave reduces the depth of the water around the engine compartment. If the water's surface reaches your tailpipe, select a gear that will maintain moderate engine revs to avoid water backing up into the exhaust; do not change gears midstream.

Crossing water deeper than thirty inches requires more extensive preparation of the vehicle and should be attempted only by experienced drivers.

Snow. The trails in this book are nearly all closed until the snow has melted or been bulldozed. Therefore, the only snow conditions that you are likely to encounter are an occasional snowdrift that has not yet melted or fresh snow from an unexpected storm. Getting through such conditions depends on the depth of the snow, its consistency, the stability of the underlying surface, and your vehicle.

If the snow is no deeper than about nine inches and there is solid ground beneath it, it should not pose a problem. In deeper snow that seems solid enough to support your vehicle, be extremely cautious: If you break through a drift, you are likely to be stuck, and if conditions are bad, you may have a long wait.

The tires you use for off-highway driving, with a wide tread pattern, are probably suitable for these snow conditions. Nonetheless, it is wise to carry chains (preferably for all four wheels) and even wiser to travel with a vehicle-mounted winch.

It is important to remember how quickly the weather can change in the Colorado high country, even in summer. Pack clothes and other items to ensure your survival if you are caught in a sudden storm.

Sand. As with most off-highway situations, your tires will affect your ability to cross sand. It is difficult to tell how well a particular tire will handle in sand just by looking at it, so be guided by the manufacturer and your dealer.

The key to driving in soft sand is floatation, which is achieved by a combination of low tire pressure and momentum. Before crossing a stretch of sand, you should start by reducing your tire pressure to between fifteen and twenty pounds. If necessary, you can safely go to as low as twelve pounds. As you cross the sand, maintain momentum so that your vehicle rides on the top of soft sand without digging in or stalling. This may require plenty of engine power.

Air the tires back up as soon as you are out of the sand to avoid damage to the tires and the rims. Airing back up requires a high-quality air compressor. Even then, it is a slow process.

The only trail in this book that may

necessitate lowering the tire pressure for sand is the Medano Pass road, which ends in the Great Sand Dunes National Monument. A refill station at the national monument is open in the peak season, which may mean that if you are down on this trail, you can avoid buying a portable compressor.

Vehicle Recovery Methods

You are sure to get stuck sooner or later. The following techniques will help you get going. The most suitable method will depend on the equipment available and the situation you are in—whether you are stuck in sand, mud, or snow, or high-centered, or unable to negotiate a hill.

Towing. Use a strong nylon yank strap, twenty to thirty feet long, two to three inches wide, rated to at least 20,000 pounds, and preferably with looped ends. This type of strap will stretch 15 to 25 percent, and the elasticity will assist in extracting the vehicle.

Attach the strap to a frame-mounted tow hook. Ensure that the driver of the stuck vehicle is ready, take up all but about six feet of slack, and then move the towing vehicle away at a moderate speed (in most circumstances this means using 4WD low range in second gear) so that the elasticity of the strap is employed in the way it is meant to be. Don't take off like a bat out of hell or you risk breaking the strap or damaging a vehicle.

Never join two yank straps together with a shackle. If one strap breaks, the shackle will become a lethal missile aimed at one of the vehicles (and anyone inside). For the same reason, never attach a yank strap to the tow ball on either vehicle.

Jacking. Jacking the vehicle may allow you to pack under the wheel (with rocks, dirt, or logs) or use your shovel to remove an obstacle. However, the standard vehicle jack is unlikely to be of as much assistance as a high-lift jack. We highly recommend purchasing a good high-lift jack as a basic accessory if you decide that you are going to do a lot of serious, off-highway, four-wheel driving.

Tire Chains. Tire chains can be of assistance in mud and snow. Link-type chains provide much more grip than cable-type chains. There are also dedicated mud chains with larger, heavier links than normal snow chains.

It is best to have chains fitted on all four wheels. However, this may not be possible since some vehicles lack sufficient clearance between the wheel and the fender. Remove chains from the front wheels as soon as practicable to avoid undue strain on the vehicle.

Be aware that it is more difficult to fit the chains after you are stuck; if at all possible try to predict their need and have them on the vehicle before trouble arises.

Winching. Most people using this book will not have a winch. But if you get serious about four-wheel driving, this is probably the first major accessory you will consider buying.

Under normal circumstances, a winch would be warranted only for the more difficult 4WD trails in this book. Having a winch is certainly comforting when you see a difficult section of road ahead and have to decide whether to risk it or turn back. Major obstacles can appear when you least expect them, even on trails that are otherwise easy.

A winch is not a panacea to all your recovery problems. Winching depends on the availability of a good anchor point, and an electric winch may not work if it is submerged in a stream. Despite these constraints, no accessory is more useful than a high-quality, powerful winch when you get into a difficult situation.

If you acquire a winch, learn to use it properly; take the time to study your owner's manual. Incorrect operation can be extremely dangerous and may cause damage to the winch or to trees, which are the most common anchors.

Navigation by the Global Positioning System (GPS)

Although this book is designed so that each trail can be navigated by simply following the detailed directions provided, nothing makes navigation easier than a GPS receiver.

The Global Positioning System (GPS)

consists of a network of twenty-four satellites, nearly thirteen thousand miles in space, in six different orbital paths. The satellites are constantly moving, making two complete orbits around the earth every twenty-four hours at about 8,500 miles per hour. Each satellite is constantly transmitting data, including its identification number, its operational health, and the date and time. It also transmits its location and the location of every other satellite in the network.

By comparing the time a signal was transmitted to the time it is received, a GPS receiver calculates how far away each satellite is. With a sufficient number of signals, the receiver can then triangulate its location. With three or more satellites, the receiver can determine latitude and longitude coordinates. With four or more, it can calculate altitude. By constantly making these calculations, it can calculate speed and direction.

The U.S. military uses the system to provide positions accurate to within half an inch. However, civilian receivers are less sophisticated and are deliberately fed slightly erroneous information in order to effectively deny military applications to hostile countries or terrorists. Because of this degradation of the signal, which is called Selective Availability (SA), the common civilian receivers have an accuracy of twenty to seventy-five yards.

A GPS receiver offers the four-wheel driver numerous benefits.

■ You can track to any point for which you know the longitude and latitude coordinates with no chance of heading in the wrong direction or getting lost. Most receivers provide an extremely easy-to-understand graphic display to keep you on track.

■ It works in all weather conditions.

■ It automatically records your route for easy backtracking.

■ You can record and name any location, so that you can relocate it with ease. This may include your campsite, a fishing spot, or even a silver mine you discover!

■ It displays your position, allowing you to pinpoint your location on a map.

■ By interfacing the GPS receiver directly to a portable computer, you can monitor and record your location as you travel (using the appropriate map software) or print the route you took.

GPS receivers have come down in price considerably in the past few years and are rapidly becoming indispensable navigational tools. Many higher-priced cars now offer integrated GPS receivers; and within the next few years, receivers will become available on most models.

Battery-powered, hand-held units that meet the needs of off-highway driving currently range from less than $100 to a little over $300 and continue to come down in price. Some high-end units feature maps that are incorporated in the display, either from a built-in database or from interchangeable memory cards. However, none of these maps currently include 4WD trails in their database.

If you are considering purchasing a GPS unit, look for the following features:

■ Price. The very cheapest units are likely outdated and very limited in their display features. Expect to pay $125 to $300.

■ The number of channels, which means the number of satellites that the unit tracks concurrently. Many older units have only one channel that switches from one satellite to another to collect the required information. Modern units have up to twelve channels, which are each dedicated to tracking one satellite. A greater number of channels provides greater accuracy, faster start-up (because the unit can acquire the initial data it needs much more rapidly), and better reception under difficult conditions (for example, if you are in a deep canyon or in dense foliage).

■ The number of routes and the number of sites (or "waypoints") per route that can be stored in memory. For off-highway use, it is important to be able to store many waypoints so that you do not have to load coordinates into the machine as frequently. Having sufficient memory also ensures that you can automatically store your location without fear that you will run out of memory.

■ It is also important that the machine can store numerous routes. GPS receivers enable you to combine waypoints to form a route, greatly simplifying navigation. As you reach each waypoint, the machine automatically swaps to the next one and directs you there.

■ The better units store up to five hundred waypoints and twenty reversible routes of up to thirty waypoints each. Also consider the number of characters a GPS receiver allows you to use in naming waypoints. When you try to recall a waypoint, you may have difficulty recognizing names restricted to only a few characters.

■ Automatic route storing. Most units automatically store your route as you go along and enable you to display it in reverse to make backtracking easy.

■ The display. Compare graphic displays. Some are much easier to decipher or offer more alternative displays.

■ The controls. Because GPS receivers have many functions, they need to have good, simple controls.

■ Vehicle mounting. To be useful, the unit needs to be located so that it can be read easily by both the driver and the navigator. Check that the unit can be conveniently located in your vehicle. Units have different shapes and mounting systems.

■ Position-format options. Maps use different grids; you should be able to display the same format on your GPS unit as on the map you are using, so that cross-referencing is simplified. There are a number of formats for latitude and longitude, as well as the UTM (Universal Transverse Mercator) grid, which is used on some maps.

After you have selected a unit, a number of optional extras are also worth considering:

■ A cigarette lighter adapter. Important because GPS units eat batteries!

■ A vehicle-mounted antenna, which will improve reception under difficult conditions. (The GPS unit can only "see" though the windows of your vehicle; it cannot monitor satellites through a metal roof.) Having a vehicle-mounted antenna also means that you do not have to consider reception when locating the receiver in your vehicle.

■ An in-car mounting system. If you are going to do a lot of touring using the GPS, you may want to attach a bracket on the dash rather than relying on a velcro mount.

■ A computer-link cable. Data from your receiver can be downloaded to your PC; or, if you have a laptop computer, you can monitor your route as you go along, using one of a number of inexpensive map software products on the market.

We used a Garmin 45 receiver to take the GPS positions in this book. This unit is now outdated, but it has served us well for the past five years in our travels throughout the United States and around the world.

Trails in the South-Central Region

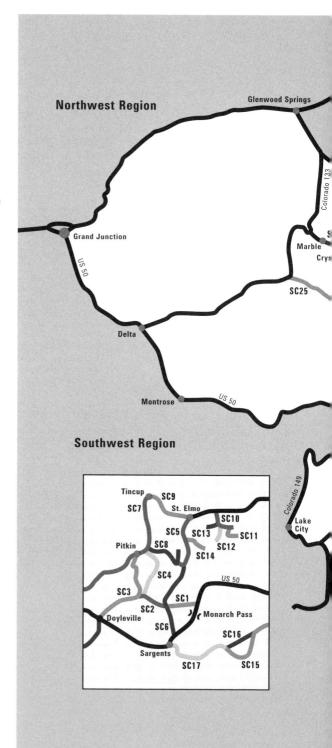

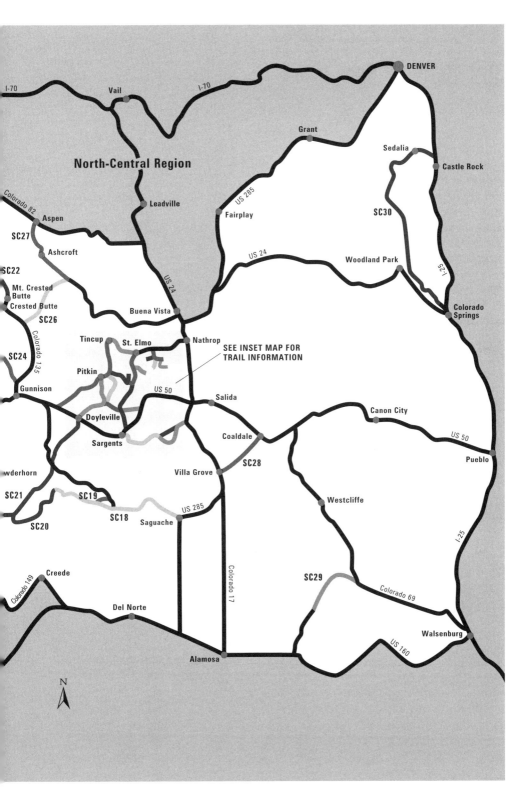

North-Central Region

DENVER

Vail

I-70

I-70

Grant

Sedalia

Castle Rock

Leadville

Colorado 82

Aspen

SC27

Fairplay

US 285

SC30

Ashcroft

SC22

Woodland Park

US 24

Mt. Crested Butte

Crested Butte

Buena Vista

SC26

US 24

I-25

Colorado Springs

Tincup

St. Elmo

Nathrop

SEE INSET MAP FOR TRAIL INFORMATION

Colorado 135

SC24

Pitkin

US 50

Gunnison

Salida

Canon City

Doyleville

Coaldale

US 50

Sargents

SC28

Pueblo

wderhorn

Villa Grove

SC21

SC19

Westcliffe

US 285

SC20

SC18

Saguache

I-25

Colorado 149

Creede

Colorado 17

SC29

Colorado 69

Del Norte

Walsenburg

N

Alamosa

US 160

Old Monarch Pass Road

STARTING POINT Intersection of US 50 and FR 237 (1 mile east of Monarch Pass)

FINISHING POINT Intersection of South-Central #6: Tomichi Pass Trail (FR 888) and FR 237

TOTAL MILEAGE 10.3 miles

UNPAVED MILEAGE 10.3 miles

DRIVING TIME 1/2 hour

ROUTE ELEVATION 11,375 to 8,900 feet

USUALLY OPEN Early June to November

DIFFICULTY RATING 1

SCENIC RATING 5

Special Attractions
■ Access to a network of 4WD trails.
■ An alternative to the main highway, US 50.

History
In 1878, eleven years before finding gold near Wagon Wheel Gap and establishing the town that was to bear his name, Nicholas Creede found silver on the east side of Monarch Pass; within months, three thousand prospectors had arrived. The discovery led to the establishment of several towns in the area, including Maysville, Garfield (originally called Junction City), and Monarch (called Chaffee City until 1884). In the same year, silver, gold, and lead were discovered in the Tomichi Valley on the west side of Monarch Pass.

In 1880, the Denver & Rio Grande Railroad built a spur line from Salida to Monarch, which continued to operate in summers until 1982. Also in 1880, a wagon road was built to serve as a stage route. This route travels from the ski area and connects with Old Monarch Pass Road. Today it is sometimes referred to as the Old, Old Monarch Pass Road. It had been open as a 4WD road but has now been closed by the Forest Service.

In the 1920s, Old Monarch Pass Road was opened, crossing the pass about one mile south of the original route. Although it was designed as a motor vehicle road, it was never paved but is still well maintained.

Following much debate about whether Marshall Pass or Monarch Pass should be used as the route for US 50, the present Monarch Pass Road was constructed in 1939. The ski area opened in the same year. When it opened, Charles Vail, the state highway engineer, named the pass after himself and had "Vail Pass" signs placed at the summit. Local residents expressed their objections to this unilateral decision by obliterating the signs with black paint. Many years later, his wish was more permanently granted along I-70.

Description
Old Monarch Pass Road (FR 237) provides a good alternative route between US 50 from the east of Monarch Pass through to the 4WD roads in the Tomichi Valley. It commences one mile east of the present summit, and the entrance is well marked. The road is graded, wide, and easy for a passenger vehicle to negotiate. There are some sections

Monarch in 1884

with steep drop-offs, but in dry conditions, these do not pose any serious problems.

The route follows a high-voltage power line through dense pine forest with only occasional stands of aspens and few expansive mountain views. It is not an unusually scenic route and the best views are at the highest point, near the main pass.

Current Road Conditions
San Isabel National Forest
Salida Ranger District
325 West Rainbow Boulevard
Salida, CO 81201
(719) 539-3591

Map References
USFS San Isabel NF
      Gunnison NF
USGS Chaffee County #3
      Gunnison County #5
The Roads of Colorado, p. 102
Trails Illustrated, #130 (incomplete), #139

Route Directions

▼ 0.0   From US 50, turn onto Monarch Pass Road (FR 237). Zero trip meter and proceed west.
10.3 ▲   End at intersection with US 50.
      GPS: N 38°30.27' W 106°19.65'

▼ 0.2 SO Road on right dead-ends in 0.3 miles.
10.1 s SO Road on left dead-ends in 0.3 miles.

▼ 1.1 SO Track on right.
9.2 ▲ SO Track on left.

▼ 1.3 SO Monarch Pass summit. Vandals had removed the plaque from the summit marker when we were there.
9.0 ▲ SO Monarch Pass summit.
      GPS: N 38°29.90' W 106°20.25'

▼ 2.8 SO Campsites on left.
7.5 ▲ SO Campsites on right.

▼ 3.3 SO Campsites on left.
7.0 ▲ SO Campsites on right.

SC Trail #1: Old Monarch Pass Road

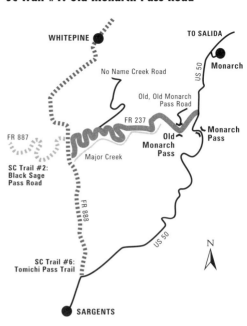

▼ 4.6 SO Track on left.
5.7 ▲ SO Track on right.

▼ 7.6 SO Track marked to Galena Gulch and No Name Creek on right. Note: This trail dead-ends due to locals putting a cable across the road about 3 miles in at GPS: N 38°30.84' W 106°23.09'. There are ruins of an old mine where the track is blocked.
2.7 ▲ SO Track marked to Galena Gulch and No Name Creek on left.
      GPS: N 38°29.88' W 106°23.76'

▼ 8.8 SO Short track on left to campsites with attractive views.
1.5 ▲ SO Short track on right to campsites with attractive views.

▼ 10.3   End at intersection with South-Central #6: Tomichi Pass Trail (FR 888).
0.0 ▲ At intersection of South-Central #6: Tomichi Pass Trail (FR 888) and FR 237, zero trip meter and proceed along FR 237 toward Old Monarch Pass.
      GPS: N 38°29.16' W 106°24.58'

FERDINAND HAYDEN: SURVEYING COLORADO

Ferdinand Vandeveer Hayden was born in Westfield, Massachusetts, on September 7, 1828, and raised on a farm near Rochester, New York, before graduating in medicine from Albany Medical College in New York.

Hayden's first expeditions were to the Dakota Badlands and the upper Missouri River into Montana from 1853 to 1857. In 1858 he undertook the geological exploration of Kansas, and in the following year he returned to Montana for a similar geological survey.

Following Civil War service as a surgeon in the Union Army, Hayden was appointed a professor at the University of Pennsylvania; but he continued his exploration of the American West, undertaking a geological survey of Nebraska in 1867.

In 1869, Hayden was placed in charge of the forerunner of the U.S. Geological Survey and made his first expedition to Colorado. During the next eight years, he was responsible for the systematic, scientific investigation of Colorado west of the Continental Divide. He directed parties of surveyors, artists, and scientists who made a detailed record of the topography of the region, including a great number of the routes that are contained in this book. He published this record in *The Geological and Geographical Atlas of Colorado and Portions of Adjacent Territory* in 1877. The information was instrumental to the settlement of Colorado and the development of railroad and mining activity.

The establishment of Yellowstone National Park in 1872 followed Hayden's survey of the area the previous year and his support for the proposal upon his return.

Hayden was an initial appointee to the U.S. Geological Survey when it was established in 1879, but was forced to retire due to ill health in 1886. He died the following year, aged fifty-nine.

Hayden Survey Party (Ferdinand Hayden is third from left)

Black Sage Pass Road

STARTING POINT Intersection of South-Central #6: Tomichi Pass Trail (FR 888) and FR 887

FINISHING POINT Intersection of South-Central #3: Waunita Pass Road (FR 763) and FR 887

TOTAL MILEAGE 6.7 miles

UNPAVED MILEAGE 6.7 miles

DRIVING TIME 1/2 hour

ROUTE ELEVATION 9,745 to 8,970 feet

USUALLY OPEN Early July to late October

DIFFICULTY RATING 1

SCENIC RATING 6

Special Attractions

- Easy road through gentle, attractive countryside.
- Access to a network of 4WD trails.

History

The Hayden survey party traveled this route between Pitkin and Whitepine. When silver was discovered near Pitkin in the late 1870s, this route provided a lower, more undulating, albeit longer, entryway to the area. By 1880, a stagecoach and numerous freight wagons were using this road daily.

In 1882, the Denver, South Park & Pacific Railroad opened the line to Pitkin through the Alpine Tunnel. The route remained in use to deliver freight from Pitkin. By this time, the resort of Waunita

Hot Springs was very popular and also needed stagecoaches and freight wagons to ferry tourists and supplies.

Subsequently, the pass was used principally for access between Whitepine and Gunnison. The stage way station at the summit of the pass continued to operate into the late 1890s.

Description

The road is accessible to passenger cars under dry conditions. It provides an easy drive through attractive ranch land and a gentle ascent to a forested summit before the scenery widens out into an open valley.

The route connects with a number of other routes in this book. To the east is Old Monarch Pass Road; and to the north are Tomichi Pass, Hancock Pass, and the Alpine Tunnel.

Current Road Conditions

Gunnison National Forest
Gunnison Ranger District
216 North Colorado
Gunnison, CO 81230
(970) 641-0471

Map References

USFS Gunnison NF
USGS Gunnison County #5
Trails Illustrated, #139
The Roads of Colorado, p. 101
Colorado Atlas & Gazetteer, pp. 59, 69

Route Directions

▼ 0.0   At intersection of South-Central #6: Tomichi Pass Trail (FR 888) and FR 887, zero trip meter and proceed west along FR 887 toward Waunita Hot Springs.

3.4 ▲   End at intersection with South-Central #6: Tomichi Pass Trail (FR 888).
       GPS: N 38°30.10′ W 106°25.26′

▼ 1.1   SO   Cattle guard.
2.3 ▲   SO   Cattle guard.

▼ 1.4   SO   Track on left to campsites.
2.0 ▲   SO   Track on right to campsites.

SC Trail #2: Black Sage Pass Road

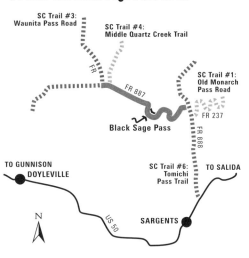

▼ 2.1   SO   Track on right.
1.3 ▲   SO   Track on left.

▼ 3.4   SO   Summit of Black Sage Pass. Zero trip meter. Cross cattle guard. Short side-road on left dead-ends in 1.2 miles. Remain on FR 887.
0.0 ▲   Continue along FR 887.
       GPS: N 38°29.46′ W 106°27.11′

▼ 0.0   Continue toward Waunita Hot Springs and Pitkin.
3.3 ▲   SO   Track on right. Cross cattle guard. Summit of Black Sage Pass. Zero trip meter.

▼ 1.6   SO   Cattle guard.
1.7 ▲   SO   Cattle guard.

▼ 3.1   TL   Intersection. South-Central #4: Middle Quartz Creek Trail is on the right.
0.2 ▲   TR   Intersection. South-Central #4: Middle Quartz Creek Trail straight on. Remain on FR 887.
       GPS: N 38°30.81′ W 106°29.61′

▼ 3.3   End at intersection with South-Central #3: Waunita Pass Road.
0.0 ▲   At intersection of FR 887 and FR 763, zero trip meter and proceed east on FR 887.
       GPS: N38°30.82′ W106°29.90′

Waunita Pass Road

STARTING POINT Pitkin
FINISHING POINT Intersection of County/FR 887 and US 50
TOTAL MILEAGE 18.7 miles
UNPAVED MILEAGE 18.7 miles
DRIVING TIME 1 hour
ROUTE ELEVATION 10,303 to 9,190 feet
USUALLY OPEN All year
DIFFICULTY RATING 1
SCENIC RATING 6

Special Attractions
- Easy road through gentle, attractive countryside.
- Access to a network of 4WD trails.

History
With the rich ore discoveries in the Monarch Pass area and on through the Tomichi Valley in 1878, stages and freight operations made regular journeys between Salida and Pitkin across Monarch, Black Sage, and Waunita Passes.

In 1880, the Denver & Rio Grande Railroad built a spur line from Salida to Monarch; and in 1882, the Alpine Tunnel railroad was opened by the Denver, South Park & Pacific Railroad, providing a railroad to Pitkin. Waunita Pass Road continued to be used

A sketch of Waunita Hot Springs Resort in 1916 showing hotel, cottages, post office, tennis courts, and bathhouses

for freight to the Tomichi Valley silver mining area. The route also provided access between Pitkin and the resort facilities at Waunita Hot Springs. However, the road was in decline from the time of the railroad.

The road passes the site of Bowerman where in 1903 J. C. Bowerman struck gold at the Independent Mine and started a rush into the area. Although newspapers heavily promoted the strike, it is doubtful that the coverage was justified by the true extent of the discovery.

Bowerman told people that his find was so rich that even a single blast could yield thousands of dollars. However, the first shipment from the Bowerman mine was postponed many times and he became secretive about the true assay of his mine and even fenced off the property. In the end, it took more than a year for him to make the first shipment, by which time a boomtown had been incorporated. By then, however, the initial enthusiasm was already on the wane.

Description
The route is generally accessible to passenger vehicles, passing through gentle valley scenery along Hot Springs Creek, then through pine and aspen forest before reaching the pass and dropping down into Pitkin.

The town site of Bowerman is on private property.

Current Road Conditions
Gunnison National Forest
Gunnison Ranger District
216 North Colorado
Gunnison, CO 81230
(970) 641-0471

Map References
USFS   Gunnison NF
USGS   Gunnison County #5
Trails Illustrated, #139
The Roads of Colorado, p. 101
Colorado Atlas & Gazetteer, pp. 59, 69

Route Directions

▼ 0.0   From the Pitkin City Hall building at
           Main and 4th Streets in Pitkin, zero trip

meter and proceed southwest.

▲ 10.4　End at the Pitkin City Hall building at
　　　　Main and 4th Streets in Pitkin.
　　　　GPS: N 38°36.48′ W 106°31.15′

▼ 0.1　TL　Onto 2nd Street.
▲ 10.3　TR　Onto Main Street.

▼ 0.2　TR　Onto State Street.
▲ 10.2　TL　Onto 2nd Street.

▼ 0.3　TL　Onto 1st Street.
▲ 10.1　TR　Onto State Street.

▼ 0.4　BR　Signpost to FR 763.
▲ 10.0　BL　Onto 1st Street.

▼ 0.5　SO　Bridge over Quartz Creek.
▲ 9.9　SO　Bridge over Quartz Creek.

▼ 1.4　SO　Cattle guard, then Gunnison National
　　　　　　Forest sign.
▲ 9.0　SO　Cattle guard.

▼ 3.3　SO　Track on right.
▲ 7.1　SO　Track on left.

▼ 3.7　SO　Track on left.
▲ 6.7　SO　Track on right.

▼ 4.6　SO　Summit of Waunita Pass. Road to
　　　　　　Wiley Gulch on left and FR 698 on
　　　　　　right.
▲ 5.8　SO　FR 698 on left and Wiley Gulch road
　　　　　　on right. Summit of Waunita Pass.
　　　　　　GPS: N 38°34.68′ W 106°30.56′

▼ 6.4　SO　Two small tracks on left.
▲ 4.0　SO　Two small tracks on right.

▼ 6.5　SO　Site of Bowerman (private property).
▲ 3.8　SO　Site of Bowerman (private property).
　　　　　　GPS: N 38°33.75′ W 106°30.69′

▼ 8.4　SO　Wiley Gulch on left.
▲ 2.0　SO　Wiley Gulch on right.

▼ 10.4　TR　Intersection. Track on the left is South-
　　　　　　Central #2: Black Sage Pass Road.
　　　　　　Zero trip meter.

SC Trail #3: Waunita Pass Road

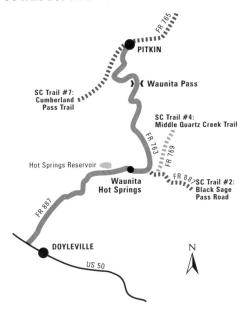

▲ 0.0　Proceed toward Pitkin on FR 763.
　　　　GPS: N 38°30.82′ W 106°29.90′

▼ 0.0　Proceed toward Waunita Hot Springs
　　　　on FR 887.
▲ 8.3　TL　T-intersection. Straight on is South-
　　　　　　Central #2: Black Sage Pass Road.
　　　　　　Zero trip meter.

▼ 0.2　SO　Cattle guard.
▲ 8.1　SO　Cattle guard.

▼ 0.4　SO　Waunita Hot Springs Ranch Resort on
　　　　　　right.
▲ 7.9　SO　Waunita Hot Springs Ranch Resort on
　　　　　　left.

▼ 2.3　SO　Track to Waunita Hot Springs
　　　　　　Reservoir on right.
▲ 6.0　SO　Track to Waunita Hot Springs
　　　　　　Reservoir on left.

▼ 2.5　SO　Track on right.
▲ 5.8　SO　Track on left.

▼ 2.6　SO　Great Horse Gulch track on right.
▲ 5.7　SO　Great Horse Gulch track on left.

▼ 2.9	SO	Short track on left.
5.4 ▲	SO	Short track on right.

▼ 3.5	SO	Bridge over Hot Springs Creek.
4.8 ▲	SO	Bridge over Hot Springs Creek.

▼ 8.3		Cattle guard and end at intersection with US 50.
0.0 ▲		At intersection of US 50 and County/FR 887, zero trip meter and proceed north on 887.

GPS: N 38°27.39' W 106°37.02'

SOUTH-CENTRAL REGION TRAIL #4

Middle Quartz Creek Trail

STARTING POINT Intersection of South-Central #2: Black Sage Pass Road (FR 887) and Waunita Hot Springs Road

FINISHING POINT Intersection of South-Central #7: Cumberland Pass Trail (FR 765) and FR 767

TOTAL MILEAGE 12.4 miles

UNPAVED MILEAGE 12.4 miles

DRIVING TIME 1 1/4 hours

ROUTE ELEVATION 11,000 to 9,025 feet

USUALLY OPEN Mid-June to late November

DIFFICULTY RATING 3

SCENIC RATING 6

Special Attractions

■ 4WD alternative to Waunita Pass Road.
■ Access to a network of 4WD roads.
■ Good camping along Middle Quartz Creek.

Description

Middle Quartz Creek Road is part of the network of forest roads on the eastern side of Waunita Pass Road. It crosses the same minor ridgeline separating the waters of Hot Springs Creek and Quartz Creek as Waunita Pass, which is about two miles to the west.

The route is a less-used alternative to Waunita Pass Road and warrants a 4WD vehicle. It is part of a network of 4WD roads that allow exploration deep into Gunnison

National Forest in areas such as Stridiron Gulch, Wiley Gulch, Canyon Creek, and the south and middle forks of Quartz Creek.

While the track is rough in spots, it should cause little difficulty in dry conditions. It offers more solitude than the more heavily used Waunita Pass Road and travels though aspen and pine forest. The scenery is attractive but lacks the spectacular views of other trails.

The area around Middle Quartz Creek offers good backcountry camping and fishing. It is surrounded with areas that offer scenic and historic day trips: historic and attractive Pitkin nearby to the west, Cumberland Pass and Tincup to the north, Brittle Silver Basin and Alpine Tunnel to the east, and Black Sage and Old Monarch Passes to the south.

Current Road Conditions

Gunnison National Forest
Gunnison Ranger District
216 North Colorado
Gunnison, CO 81230
(970) 641-0471

Map References

USFS Gunnison NF
USGS Gunnison County #5
Trails Illustrated, #130
The Roads of Colorado, p. 101
Colorado Atlas & Gazetteer, p. 59

Route Directions

▼ 0.0		From T-intersection of South-Central #2: Black Sage Pass Road (FR 887) and FR 774 to Middle Quartz Creek, zero trip meter and proceed east along FR 774.
12.4 ▲		End at T-intersection with South-Central #2: Black Sage Pass Road (FR 887). South-Central #3: Waunita Pass Road is straight on 0.2 miles.

GPS: N 38°30.81' W 106°29.61'

▼ 0.3	BL	Track on right dead-ends.
12.1 ▲	BR	Track on left dead-ends.

▼ 0.7	BR	FR 774 on left. Follow FR 769.
11.7 ▲	BL	FR 774 on right. Follow FR 769.

▼ 1.3   SO   Waunita walking track on right.
11.1 ▲   SO   Waunita walking track on left.
        GPS: N 38°31.60' W 106°28.88'

▼ 2.4   SO   Track on right.
10.0 ▲   SO   Track on left.

▼ 2.8   SO   Track on right (unmarked).
9.6 ▲   SO   Track on left (unmarked).

▼ 3.2   BR   Intersection. Sign on right points to Hicks Gulch behind and Buffalo Fork straight ahead. Sign on the left marks track to Stridiron Creek.
9.2 ▲   BL   Intersection. Hicks Gulch straight. Track to Stridiron Creek on right.
        GPS: N 38°32.80' W 106°28.13'

▼ 3.3   SO   Trail on right.
9.1 ▲   SO   Trail on left.

▼ 4.8   BL   Fork in the road. Canyon Creek Trailhead is to the right. Follow road left toward Middle Quartz Creek.
7.6 ▲   BR   Canyon Creek Trailhead is to the left.
        GPS: N 38°34.06' W 106°28.23'

▼ 6.4   SO   Track on right, then track on left. Remain on FR 769.
6.0 ▲   SO   Track on left, then track on right. Remain on FR 769.
        GPS: N 38°34.67' W 106°27.86'

▼ 7.1   BR   Track on left.
5.3 ▲   BL   Track on right.
        GPS: N 38°34.80' W 106°28.36'

▼ 7.6   TR   Fork in the road, FR 769 to the right; FR 779 to the left.
4.8 ▲   BL   Remain on FR 769. FR 779 on the right.
        GPS: N 38°35.22' W 106°28.25'

▼ 9.7   TR   Intersection with FR 769 to the right; FR 779 to the left.
2.7 ▲   TL   Remain on FR 769. FR 779 on the right.
        GPS: N 38°35.71' W 106°28.55'

▼ 10.3   SO   Cross over creek.

SC Trail #4: Middle Quartz Creek Trail

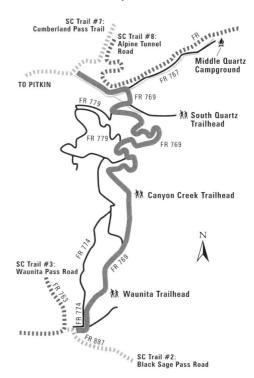

2.1 ▲   SO   Cross over creek.

▼ 10.4   SO   Track on right leads to South Quartz Trailhead walking track.
2.0 ▲   SO   Track on left leads to South Quartz Trailhead walking track.

▼ 10.7   TL   Cross over creek, then intersection with Middle Quartz Creek Road (FR 767). Middle Quartz Creek Campground to the right and Pitkin to the left.
1.7 ▲   TR   Intersection with FR 769.
        GPS: N 38°36.19' W 106°28.07'

▼ 12.4   End at intersection with South-Central #7: Cumberland Pass Trail (FR 765). Pitkin is to the left and Tincup to the right.
0.0 ▲   At intersection of South-Central #7: Cumberland Pass Trail (FR 765) and FR 767, zero trip meter and proceed east along FR 767.
        GPS: N 38°36.72' W 106°29.68'

Hancock Pass Trail

STARTING POINT St. Elmo

FINISHING POINT Intersection with South-Central #8: Alpine Tunnel Road (FR 839) and FR 888

TOTAL MILEAGE 9.3 miles

UNPAVED MILEAGE 9.3 miles

DRIVING TIME 1 1/4 hours

ROUTE ELEVATION 12,250 to 9,980 feet

USUALLY OPEN Early July to October

DIFFICULTY RATING 4 (5 if traveling toward St. Elmo)

SCENIC RATING 9

Special Attractions

- St. Elmo township and the sites of Hancock and Romley.
- Spectacular summit views of Brittle Silver Basin.
- Hiking trail to the east portal of the Alpine Tunnel.
- Moderately difficult 4WD route.
- Access to a network of 4WD trails.

History

The history of the Hancock Pass crossing is poorly documented, perhaps because of the confusion between this pass and Williams Pass, which is located a couple of miles further north. Hancock Pass was used as a mining route in the 1880s but has never been an important commercial route. It was not officially named until 1962. Much of the route on the east side of the pass follows the old Denver, South Park & Pacific railway grade toward the Alpine Tunnel.

This trip originates at one of the most-photographed and best-preserved ghost towns in Colorado: St. Elmo (see box).

The route passes the town site of Romley founded in the late 1870s for the workers of the nearby Mary Murphy and Pat Murphy Mines.

The Mary Murphy Mine was by far the biggest mine in the Alpine district. It is said to be named after a kind nurse in Denver who once cared for the prospector who discovered the mine. The Mary Murphy grew so large that it supported Romley, St. Elmo, and Hancock, making the region quite prosperous.

When the Denver, South Park & Pacific Railroad came through Romley in 1881, a five-thousand-foot tramway was built to transfer ore to the railroad cars. In 1908, tragedy struck when sparks from a train engine kindled a fire that reduced most of Romley to ashes. When the town was rebuilt, the buildings were painted bright red with white trim, although nobody knows why!

The Mary Murphy Mine, which continued to operate until 1926, is located on the road to Pomeroy Lakes (South-Central #14). In 1982, the mining company destroyed the buildings that remained in the deserted town.

The Denver, South Park & Pacific

Above: the Allie Belle Mine building in 1950
Below: the precarious position of the building today

ST. ELMO

St Elmo was established in 1880 and incorporated under the name of Forest City. The post office soon insisted that the name be changed to St. Elmo, because other towns had been named Forest City.

St. Elmo grew with the success of the Mary Murphy Mine and several other mines in the vicinity. It became a major supply center within the district and served as a convenient stopover for travelers to Tincup, Alpine, and various other mountain passes nearby. Before the railroad's arrival, St. Elmo was a stage stop. With the opening of the Alpine Tunnel by the Denver, South Park & Pacific Railroad in 1882, St. Elmo became a main station on the line.

St. Elmo's main street around 1880

In its heyday, St. Elmo was a thriving town with a population of about 1,500 and served as a supply center for the numerous mining camps in the area. It had five hotels, a newspaper, and many other businesses. Although nearby towns had saloons, St. Elmo was considered the best place to spend a Saturday night. The construction workers on the Alpine Tunnel came to St. Elmo for their weekend sprees.

Fire swept through the town in 1890, causing much damage. Two blocks in the business district burned and were never rebuilt.

After a portion of the tunnel collapsed in 1910, it never reopened. Heavy snow removal, unstable silver prices and lack of freight were all contributing reasons for the management to discontinue service through the Alpine Tunnel. By 1926, it was no longer profitable to continue rail service to St. Elmo. A few residents continued to live in the area, hoping that mining would revive.

By the mid-1950s only two residents remained in the town: Tony and Annabelle Stark, who grew up in St. Elmo and operated a general store (which still stands) from the boom years. They stayed on long after the town faded, living in isolation during the long winters and opening their store to tourists in the summer. After the Starks passed away, St. Elmo assumed the role of a true ghost town.

St. Elmo is one of the best-preserved mining towns in Colorado, with most of the buildings along its main street looking much the same as they did a hundred years ago. It is listed on the National Register of Historic Places and has been the subject of a Historic American Building survey. St. Elmo is a must-see for visitors who want to step back into a wild-West mining town of the 1800s.

Railroad established the town of Hancock in 1880 to support the construction of the Alpine Tunnel. It was named for the Hancock Placer, the first claim in the area. Most of the hundreds of workers employed to build the tunnel lived in Hancock. With five general stores, a hotel, several saloons and restaurants, and two sawmills cutting lumber for the tunnel and railroad, the town supported a population of close to one thousand.

After the Alpine Tunnel was completed in 1881, Hancock became a station on the line to Pitkin. Main Street faced the railroad tracks. The population declined substantially when the tunnel was completed, but many workers were still needed to keep the tracks clear of heavy snow. Large crews labored constantly throughout winter months.

Hancock's population continued to dwindle when many of the area mines closed down, but the big decline occurred after 1910 when the Alpine Tunnel caved in. Hancock became a true ghost town. All the buildings have now collapsed, although the structures and foundations are clearly visible in the meadow. The last to fall away was a saloon and the remains of it and other buildings are still evident.

Description

Romley is located about 2.5 miles from St. Elmo. Shortly past Romley is the turnoff for the road to Pomeroy Lakes, which goes past the Mary Murphy Mine.

At the 4.8-mile point is one of the most precarious-looking structures you are likely to see. The building, which looks as though it will slide into the middle of the road at any moment, once stored ore produced by the Allie Belle Mine while it was waiting to be loaded into rail trucks. Despite appearances, the building has been cantilevered this way for years and is presumably quite sound. A number of other mine buildings are located above this structure. A huge rock has rolled down the hill and crashed through the back wall of a miner's cabin—we hope not while he was in residence!

Not far past the leaning storage shed lies the town site of Hancock.

Just past Hancock, there is a parking lot at the start of the hiking trail to the Atlantic railway station, which was located at the eastern end of the Alpine Tunnel. Before 1992, this road was open to vehicles, but a landslide blocked it that year, leaving as the only access a 2.5-mile hike along the old railway grade.

Shortly after the parking lot, there is an intersection. Turn right and continue on the trail to Hancock Pass. Bear left to a 1.4-mile road to Hancock Lakes Trailhead (GPS coordinates: N 38°37.18' W 106°21.29'). A half-mile walk from the trailhead are the picturesque Hancock Lakes.

Until this intersection, the route is an easy 2WD road and suitable for passenger vehicles. However, from this point on, the road becomes progressively tougher and is rated 4WD.

The summit of the pass provides a spectacular view of Brittle Silver Basin and the ridge of thirteen-thousand-foot peaks beyond. The Tomichi Pass shelf road is clearly visible, clinging to the southern ridge surrounding the basin.

From the summit, the remaining mile of road descends steeply into Brittle Silver Basin. For the last hundred yards, loose rocks make getting traction a little difficult, especially if you are going uphill toward the pass.

Current Road Conditions

Gunnison National Forest
Gunnison Ranger District
216 North Colorado
Gunnison, CO 81230
(970) 641-0471

Map References

USFS   Gunnison NF or San Isabel NF
USGS   Chaffee County #2
          Chaffee County #3
          Gunnison County #5
Trails Illustrated, #130
The Roads of Colorado, p. 102
Colorado Atlas & Gazetteer, p. 59

Route Directions

▼ 0.0   At Miner's Exchange general store in St. Elmo, zero trip meter and proceed east out of St. Elmo on County 162.
5.7 ▲   End at Miner's Exchange general store in St. Elmo.
          GPS: N 38°42.23' W 106°20.65'

▼ 0.3   TR Onto County/FR 295 toward Hancock.
5.4 ▲   TL Onto County 162 toward St. Elmo.

▼ 0.8   SO San Isabel National Forest Service board sign on right.
4.9 ▲   SO San Isabel National Forest Service board sign on left.

▼ 2.4   SO Cross through creek.
3.3 ▲   SO Cross though creek.

▼ 2.5   SO Romley on right.
3.2 ▲   SO Romley on left.

▼ 3.1   BR Road forks.
2.6 ▲   SO Track on right.

▼ 3.3   SO South-Central #14: Pomeroy Lakes and Mary Murphy Mine Trail is on left.
2.4 ▲   SO Track on right to Pomeroy Lakes and Mary Murphy Mine.
        GPS: N 38°40.38′ W 106°21.95′

▼ 4.8   SO Old ore storage house for the Allie Belle Mine on left, a precariously perched building overhanging the road.
0.9 ▲   SO Ore storage house for the Allie Belle Mine on right.
        GPS: N 38°39.08′ W 106°22.07′

▼ 5.5   SO Hancock town site.
0.2 ▲   SO Hancock town site.
        GPS: N 38°38.40′ W 106°21.64′

▼ 5.6   BL Cross over creek, then fork in road. Follow sign to Hancock Pass and Hancock Lakes. Track on right is parking for walking track to the Alpine Tunnel east portal.
0.1 ▲   BR Left is parking area. Bear right toward Hancock, then cross over creek.

▼ 5.7   TR U-turn onto FR 299 toward Hancock Pass. (SO goes to Hancock Lakes Trailhead.) Zero trip meter.
0.0 ▲   Proceed toward Hancock.
        GPS: N 38°38.27′ W 106°21.63′

▼ 0.0   Proceed along FR 299.
3.6 ▲   TL U-turn left goes to Hancock. Right goes to Hancock Lakes. Zero trip meter.

▼ 1.5   SO Track on right to mine.
2.1 ▲   SO Track on left to mine.

▼ 1.9-2.0 SO Mine portals on right along the road.
1.6-1.7 ▲ SO Mine portals on left along the road.

▼ 2.0   SO Hancock Pass sign is slightly before

SC Trail #5: Hancock Pass Trail

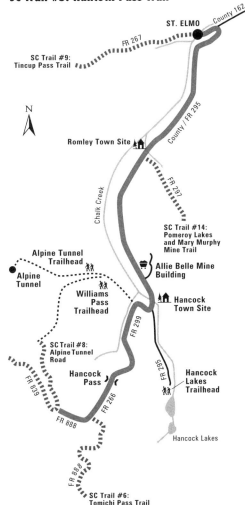

the summit. After crest, road is now named FR 266.
1.6 ▲   SO Hancock Pass sign is slightly past the summit. After crest, road is now named FR 299.
        GPS: N 38°37.31′ W 106°22.44′

▼ 2.9   SO Rough and rocky shallow crossing through creek. Remains of old cabin on right.
0.7 ▲   SO Remains of old cabin on left. Cross through creek.

▼ 3.0   TR Intersection. Left to Tomichi Pass (FR 888) and right to Pitkin.

| 0.6 | BL | Intersection. FR 888 continues to Tomichi Pass. Follow road to Hancock Pass (FR 266). |
| | | **GPS: N 38°36.69' W 106°22.69'** |

▼ 3.6	End at intersection with South-Central #8: Alpine Tunnel Road (FR 839).
0.0 ▲	At intersection of South-Central #8: Alpine Tunnel Road (FR 839) and FR 888, zero trip meter and proceed along FR 888.
	GPS: N 38°36.83' W 106°23.37'

SOUTH-CENTRAL REGION TRAIL #6

Tomichi Pass Trail

STARTING POINT Intersection of South-Central #5: Hancock Pass Trail (FR 266) and FR 888

FINISHING POINT Intersection of FR 888 and US 50

TOTAL MILEAGE 15.9 miles

UNPAVED MILEAGE 12.1 miles

DRIVING TIME 2 hours

ROUTE ELEVATION 12,020 to 8,600 feet

USUALLY OPEN Early July to October

DIFFICULTY RATING 5

SCENIC RATING 9

Special Attractions

■ A challenging 4WD trail.
■ Wonderful summit views of Brittle Silver Basin and Hancock Pass Trail.
■ Town sites of Tomichi and Whitepine.
■ Access to a network of 4WD trails.

History

"Tomichi" is the Ute word for hot water, a reference to the many hot springs in the area.

The main access to the mining areas of Tomichi and Whitepine was southeast to Monarch via Old Monarch Pass or west to Gunnison via Black Sage Pass. From the late 1870s this entire area was teeming with miners, and Tomichi Pass Road was built to provide access north from the mining settlements of Tomichi and Whitepine to the

Denver, South Park & Pacific Railroad and the towns of Pitkin and, via Hancock Pass, St. Elmo. However, the route was too high and difficult to be developed much beyond a pack trail, although wagons did use it when road and weather conditions allowed.

Tomichi was laid out because of silver finds in the area in 1880. Before long, the town's population swelled to nearly 1,500. A smelter was constructed to serve the Magna Charta Tunnel, the best producing silver mine in the area, and the other local mines. Unfortunately, it was destroyed by fire in 1883. The silver crash in 1893 drastically reduced the town's population. All the nearby mines were closed except the Eureka, which operated until 1895. In 1899, a huge avalanche struck the town, destroying all the buildings and mine machinery. Five or six people were killed, and all survivors abandoned the site.

Prospectors began arriving in Whitepine in 1879, and the town was founded in 1880 and thrived throughout the 1880s. Its population reached about three thousand, but despite high expectations, none of the area mines produced much, and with the silver

A plank bridge over a muddy section of Tomichi Pass Trail

A view of the Tomichi Pass 4WD trail from Hancock Pass

crash of 1893, the town was doomed. By the following year, Whitepine was virtually deserted.

The town saw a brief resurgence of activity in 1901 and staged a more lasting comeback when lead, zinc, and copper were mined during World Wars I and II, mainly at the Akron Mine. The Akron Mine hit a high point in 1948, when it reached production of one hundred tons per day. In 1946 Whitepine opened a ski area with an 1,800-foot rope tow but after just two years, the tow was dismantled and moved. Whitepine is now primarily a summer residence, with many reconstructed miners' cabins.

The Whitepine and Tomichi stage line serviced the two towns with regular stages to Sargents from 1881. At Sargents, passengers could connect with the Denver & Rio Grande Railroad, which reached town that year following the completion of the line across Marshall Pass.

Description

Tomichi Pass Trail remains one of the more difficult roads in the area. On the north side of the pass, the road crosses a plank bridge over boggy ground before climbing a very narrow shelf that can be blocked by talus slides. It may be necessary to clear the road in order to pass safely. The road is certainly better suited to a smaller 4WD vehicle; but we have traveled it both ways in a Suburban, so it is possible to safely negotiate it in a full-sized vehicle. The wrecked 4WD vehicle below the road serves as a cautionary billboard for the reckless.

The summit provides a wonderful view back to Hancock Pass Trail.

On the south side of the pass, the road begins a long, fairly gentle descent, with narrow sections where passing another vehicle is difficult. The road surface is rough but is mainly imbedded rock and provides a sound footing. People who are afraid of heights will be pleased to know that drop-offs along this road are mostly restricted to the immediate vicinity of the summit of the pass.

Once the road descends below timberline, it becomes smoother and easier. About three miles after the pass, the road goes through the old Tomichi Cemetery. This heavily forested site is all that remains of the Tomichi township.

From Whitepine, the road may be negotiated in a car.

SC Trail #6:
Tomichi Pass Trail

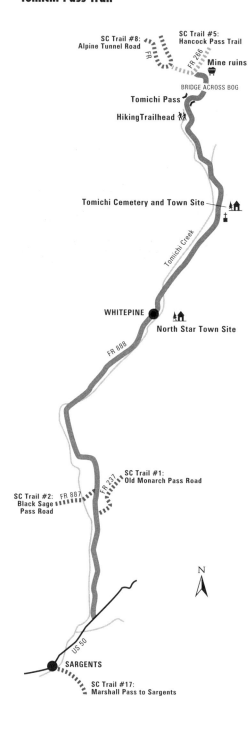

Current Road Conditions
Gunnison National Forest
Gunnison Ranger District
216 North Colorado
Gunnison, CO 81230
(970) 641-0471

Map References
USFS Gunnison NF
USGS Gunnison County #5
Trails Illustrated, #130, #139
The Roads of Colorado, p. 102
Colorado Atlas & Gazetteer, pp. 59, 69

Route Directions

▼ 0.0 From intersection of FR 266 and FR 888, zero trip meter and proceed along FR 888 toward Tomichi.

15.9 ▲ End at intersection with South-Central #5: Hancock Pass Trail (FR 266). Straight ahead leads to South-Central #8: Alpine Tunnel Road.
GPS: N 38°36.69′ W 106°22.69′

▼ 0.3 SO Interesting mine with several old buildings, an old boiler and open portal.

15.6 ▲ SO Interesting mine with several old buildings, an old boiler and open portal.
GPS: N 38°36.62′ W 106°22.46′

▼ 0.8 SO Plank bridge over boggy area.

15.1 ▲ SO Plank bridge over boggy area.

▼ 1.1 SO Summit of Tomichi Pass.

14.8 ▲ SO Summit of Tomichi Pass.
GPS: N 38°36.20′ W 106°22.95′

▼ 1.3 SO Walking trail on right to Canyon Creek, South Quartz, Horseshoe Creek.

14.6 ▲ SO Walking trail on left to Canyon Creek, South Quartz, Horseshoe Creek.

▼ 1.9 SO Cross through creek.

14.0 ▲ SO Cross through creek.

▼ 2.0 SO Cross through creek.

13.9 ▲ SO Cross through creek.

| ▼ 2.4 | SO | Cross through creek. |
| 13.5 ▲ | SO | Cross through creek. |

| ▼ 2.6 | SO | Cross through creek. |
| 13.3 ▲ | SO | Cross through creek. |

| ▼ 2.9 | SO | Cross through creek. |
| 13.0 ▲ | SO | Cross through creek. |

| ▼ 3.4 | SO | Cross through creek. |
| 12.5 ▲ | SO | Cross through creek. |

| ▼ 4.0 | SO | Tomichi Cemetery on left. Bear right at intersection with 8881.C. |
| 11.9 ▲ | SO | Tomichi Cemetery on right. Bear left. |

GPS: N 38°34.26' W 106°22.19'

| ▼ 4.1 | SO | Cross through creek. |
| 11.8 ▲ | SO | Cross through creek. |

| ▼ 4.2 | SO | Track on left. |
| 11.7 ▲ | SO | Track on right. |

| ▼ 4.3 | SO | Track on left. |
| 11.6 ▲ | SO | Track on right. |

| ▼ 4.4 | TL | Track on right is a dead end. Turn toward Whitepine. |
| 11.5 ▲ | TR | Track on left is a dead end. Turn toward Tomichi Pass. |

GPS: N 38°34.06' W 106°22.44'

| ▼ 6.1 | SO | Bridge over Tomichi Creek. |
| 9.8 ▲ | SO | Bridge over Tomichi Creek. |

| ▼ 6.5 | SO | Town of Whitepine. |
| 9.4 ▲ | SO | Town of Whitepine. |

GPS: N 38°32.59' W 106°23.57'

| ▼ 6.8 | SO | Mine and mill on left. |
| 9.1 ▲ | SO | Mine and mill on right. |

| ▼ 8.4 | SO | USFS Snowblind Campground on left. |
| 7.5 ▲ | SO | USFS Snowblind Campground on right. |

| ▼ 10.0 | SO | Intersection with South-Central #2: Black Sage Pass Road (FR 887) to the right. |
| 5.9 ▲ | SO | Intersection with South-Central #2: Black Sage Pass Road (FR 887) to the left. |

GPS: N 38°30.11' W 106°25.25'

| ▼ 11.4 | SO | South-Central #1: Old Monarch Pass Road on left. |
| 4.5 ▲ | SO | South-Central #1: Old Monarch Pass Road on right. |

| ▼ 12.1 | SO | Paved road. |
| 3.8 ▲ | SO | Unpaved. |

| ▼ 15.9 | | End at intersection with US 50. |
| 0.0 ▲ | | At intersection of US 50 and FR 888, zero trip meter and proceed along FR 888 toward Whitepine. |

GPS: N 38°25.40 W 106°24.36'

SOUTH-CENTRAL REGION TRAIL #7

Cumberland Pass Trail

STARTING POINT Tincup
FINISHING POINT Pitkin
TOTAL MILEAGE 15.6 miles
UNPAVED MILEAGE 15.2 miles
DRIVING TIME 1 1/2 hours
ROUTE ELEVATION 12,015 to 9,190 feet
USUALLY OPEN Early July to late September
DIFFICULTY RATING 3
SCENIC RATING 10

Special Attractions

- The historic and attractive town of Tincup, one of the wildest towns of the old West.
- Tincup Cemetery.
- Access to a multitude of side roads near the summit.
- Spectacular, panoramic summit views.
- Bon Ton Mine, with its deserted cabins and mine buildings.

History

The main road was built in 1882, upgrading an earlier pack trail. Until this time, Tincup had received the majority of its supplies across the gentler slopes of Cottonwood

Tincup in 1916

Pass. However, when the Denver, South Park & Pacific Railroad reached Pitkin in 1882, it became necessary to have a good freight route from Tincup to Quartz, the major depot established by the railroad two-and-one-half miles north of Pitkin.

Description

The main road over Cumberland Pass is one of the highest 2WD roads in the United States. This 4WD road takes an alternative, more direct, but slower route from Tincup to the north side of the pass.

The route leaves Tincup and travels past the old cemetery, which consists of four grassy knolls. One was for Catholics, one for Protestants, and another for Jews; the fourth —and largest—is the boot hill section, which was reserved as the final resting place for those who died with their boots on and guns blazing. The size of boot hill is a reflection of Tincup's notoriety as one of the wildest towns of the old West.

This route turns off from the main Cumberland Pass road at the 0.3-mile point. The turnoff is unmarked and not easily noticed. As it climbs toward the pass, the road passes numerous abandoned mines, rusting mining machinery, and decaying

cabins as it winds through the pine trees. Although it is narrow in sections and has some loose surfaces, the road provides no particular difficulty in dry conditions.

As the road ascends above timberline, magnificent panoramic views open up and numerous 4WD trails crisscross the area. Staying on the correct trail can be tricky in this section; fortunately, the summit is visible, and most trails allow you to head in that direction. Because so many people use these roads, it is especially important to Tread Lightly! and remain on the trails open to 4WD vehicles.

Bon Ton Mine ruins

At the summit, the high peaks of the Sawatch Range dominate the skyline to the east, the Elk Mountains are in the distance to the west, and the Willow Creek Valley is to the north, with the main 2WD road to Tincup visible as it descends into the valley.

The descent toward Pitkin is along a well-maintained 2WD road. It passes through the remains of the Bon Ton Mine, which has numerous old cabins. The mine commenced operations around 1910 but found its greatest success when it switched to molybdenum production.

Five miles past the Bon Ton is the turnoff for the Alpine Tunnel and Tomichi and Hancock Passes.

Current Road Conditions

Gunnison National Forest
Gunnison Ranger District
216 North Colorado
Gunnison, CO 81230
(970) 641-0471

Map References

USFS   Gunnison NF
USGS   Gunnison County #5
      Gunnison County #3
Trails Illustrated, #130
The Roads of Colorado, p. 101
Colorado Atlas & Gazetteer, p. 59

Route Directions

▼ 0.0   Start at intersection of Mirror Lake Road (FR 267) and Cumberland Pass Road (FR 765) in Tincup. Zero trip meter and proceed south.

4.9 ▲   End at intersection with Mirror Lake Road (FR 267), which is also South-Central #9: Tincup Pass Trail.
      GPS: N 38°45.27' W 106°28.77'

▼ 0.1   SO   Cross bridge.
4.8 ▲   SO   Cross bridge.

▼ 0.2   SO   FR 765.2A to Tincup Cemetery on left.
4.7 ▲   SO   FR 765.2A to Tincup Cemetery on right.

▼ 0.3   TL   Turn onto unmarked turnoff on

left, FR 765.2B.
4.6 ▲   TR   Turn onto FR 765 toward Tincup.
      GPS: N 38°44.98' W 106°28.83'

▼ 2.1   TL   Intersection.
2.8 ▲   TR   Intersection.
      GPS: N 38°43.57' W 106°28.73'

▼ 2.3   SO   Private cottages on left.
2.6 ▲   SO   Private cottages on right.
      GPS: N 38°43.37' W 106°28.78'

▼ 2.5   BL   Track on right.
2.4 ▲   BR   Track on left.
      GPS: N 38°43.19' W 106°28.70'

▼ 2.6   SO   Mine on left, building ruins, and tailing dump.
2.3 ▲   SO   Mine on right, building ruins, and tailing dump.

▼ 2.6   BR   Track on left.
2.3 ▲   BL   Track on right.

▼ 2.6 TL/TR   S-turn.
2.2 ▲ TR/TL   S-turn.
      GPS: N 38°43.12' W 106°28.70'

▼ 2.7   SO   Track on left. Abandoned mine machinery.
2.1 ▲   SO   Track on right. Abandoned mine machinery.
      GPS: N 38°43.04' W 106°28.71'

▼ 2.9   BL   Fork in road.
2.0 ▲   BR   Track on left.
      GPS: N 38°42.87' W 106°28.68'

▼ 3.0   BL   Fork in road.
1.9 ▲   BR   Fork in road

▼ 3.1 SO/BR Track on right to several cabin ruins. Then bear right at fork in road.
1.8 ▲ BL/BR Track on right. Track on left to cabin ruins.
      GPS: N 38°42.75' W 106°28.65'

▼ 3.2   SO   Track on right. Track on left.
1.7 ▲   SO   Track on left. Track on right.

SC Trail #7:
Cumberland Pass Trail

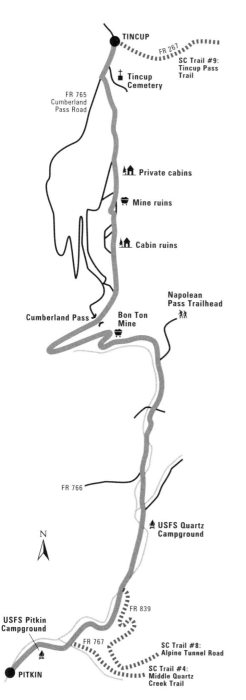

▼ 3.4	BR	Fork in road.
1.5 ▲	BL	Fork in road.
		GPS: N 38°42.47 W 106°28.70'

| ▼ 3.4 | SO | Track on right. |
| 1.4 ▲ | SO | Track on left. |

| ▼ 3.5 | BL | Track on right. |
| 1.4 ▲ | BR | Track on left. |

| ▼ 4.1 | BR | Fork in road. |
| 0.8 ▲ | BL | Fork in road. |

| ▼ 4.5 | BR | Fork in road. |
| 30 yds ▲ | BL | Fork in road. |

| ▼ 30 yds | BL | Fork in road. |
| 0.4 ▲ | BR | Fork in road. |

▼ 4.9	TL	Cumberland Pass summit and intersection with Cumberland Pass Road. Zero trip meter at summit marker.
0.0 ▲		Proceed along 765.2B.
		GPS: N 38°41.37' W 106°29.03'

| ▼ 0.0 | | Continue south on FR 765 toward Pitkin. |
| 7.9 ▲ | TR | Cumberland Pass summit. Zero trip meter at summit marker and shortly after turn right onto 4WD track (FR 765.2B). |

| ▼ 0.6 | SO | 4WD track on right. |
| 7.3 ▲ | SO | 4WD track on left. |

| ▼ 0.9 | SO | 4WD track on right. |
| 7.0 ▲ | SO | 4WD track on left. |

| ▼ 1.0 | UT | Track on right. |
| 6.9 ▲ | UT | Track on left. |

| ▼ 1.3 | SO | 4WD track on left. |
| 6.6 ▲ | SO | 4WD track on right. |

▼ 2.8	SO	Bon Ton Mine on left and cluster of old mine buildings.
5.0 ▲	SO	Bon Ton Mine on right and cluster of old mine buildings.
		GPS: N 38°40.97' W 106°28.80'

| ▼ 4.0 | SO | Track on left leads to Napoleon |

Pass Trailhead.

3.8 ▲ SO Track on right leads to Napoleon Pass
         Trailhead.

▼ 4.9 SO Tracks on right and left.
2.9 ▲ SO Tracks on left and right.

▼ 5.3 SO Cross North Quartz Creek.
2.5 ▲ SO Cross North Quartz Creek.

▼ 5.5 SO Track on right.
2.3 ▲ SO Track on left.

▼ 5.9 SO FR 766 to Hall's Gulch on right.
1.9 ▲ SO FR 766 to Hall's Gulch on left.
         GPS: N 38°39.07' W 106°28.15'

▼ 6.6 SO Track on left to Mosquito Creek.
1.3 ▲ SO Track on right to Mosquito Creek.

▼ 6.9 SO USFS Quartz Campground on left.
1.0 ▲ SO USFS Quartz Campground on right.

▼ 7.9 SO Town site of Quartz. South-Central #8:
         Alpine Tunnel Road (FR 839) on left.
         Zero trip meter.
0.0 ▲   Proceed along FR 765 toward
         Cumberland Pass.
         GPS: N 38°37.49' W 106°28.52'

▼ 0.0   Proceed along FR 765 toward Pitkin.
2.9 ▲ SO Town site of Quartz. South-Central #8:
         Alpine Tunnel Road (FR 839) on right.
         Zero trip meter.

▼ 1.5 SO South-Central #4: Middle Quartz Creek
         Trail (FR 767) on left.
1.4 ▲ SO South-Central #4: Middle Quartz Creek
         Trail (FR 767) on right.

▼ 1.9 SO Seasonal gate, then USFS Pitkin
         Campground on left.
1.0 ▲ SO USFS Pitkin Campground on right, then
         seasonal gate.

▼ 2.4 TR Stop sign at intersection of State and
         9th Streets in Pitkin. Silver Plume
         General Store.
0.5 ▲ TL Onto FR 765.

▼ 2.5 TL Onto Main Street.
0.4 ▲ TR Onto 9th Street.

▼ 2.9   End at Pitkin City Hall at intersection of
         Main Street (County 76) and 4th Street.
0.0 ▲   In front of the Pitkin City Hall at the
         intersection of Main Street (County 76)
         and 4th Street, zero trip meter and pro-
         ceed northeast along Main Street.
         GPS: N 38°36.50' W 106°31.14'

Alpine Tunnel Road

STARTING POINT Intersection of Alpine Tunnel
   Road (FR 839) and Cumberland Pass
   Road (FR 765) at Quartz town site
FINISHING POINT Alpine Station
TOTAL MILEAGE 9.5 miles
UNPAVED MILEAGE 9.5 miles
DRIVING TIME 3/4 hour (one-way)
ROUTE ELEVATION 11,597 to 11,180 feet
USUALLY OPEN Early July to September
DIFFICULTY RATING 1
SCENIC RATING 10

Special Attractions
■ The restored Alpine Station.
■ The Palisades section of the old railroad
  grade.
■ Railroad water tanks.
■ Town sites of Quartz and Woodstock and
  the site of the Sherrod Loop.

History
Two railroads waged a battle to be the first to
connect the Gunnison area to Denver. The
Denver & Rio Grande Railroad chose
Marshall Pass as its route, so the owner of the
Denver, South Park & Pacific Railroad, for-
mer governor John Evans, financed a project
to tunnel through the Sawatch Range.

A tunnel through the Continental Divide
seemed a shorter and more strategic route.
Bids were opened to build the Alpine Tunnel
in 1879. The bore through the mountain
was to be 1,800 feet long. However, the rail-

road underestimated the severity of the weather, the geologic rock formations at the site, and the difficulty of working at the 11,600-foot altitude, with wind gusts to fifty miles per hour and temperatures at forty degrees below zero.

In 1880, work began, and five hundred laborers worked day and night. Work camps were established at each end of the tunnel. Severe weather conditions and poor working conditions created and exacerbated gigantic labor problems. Workers walked off the site in droves when they experienced the high winds and freezing temperatures they were expected to endure. The railroad recruited workers from the East and Midwest by offering free transportation to Colorado. More than one hundred thousand men were employed, and many worked only a day or two before leaving. Sometimes the entire crew threatened to quit en masse.

The tunnel was bored by July 1881, almost a year behind schedule (which had allowed only six months to complete the project). When the competing Denver & Rio Grande reached Gunnison in early August, the discouraged Denver, South Park & Pacific Railroad company halted the Alpine Tunnel project for about six months. Finally, work continued, and the first train passed through the tunnel in December 1881.

Alpine station circa 1900

The Alpine Station was developed at the west, or Pacific, end of the tunnel, with a bunkhouse where track workers lived, a storehouse, and a section house. The section house included a kitchen, a dining room, a pantry, and several bedrooms. A large stone engine house was built at the station in 1881. Aside from holding six engines, the engine house also contained a large coal bin and a water tank with a 9,516-gallon capacity, a turntable, and a locomotive service area. In 1883, a telegraph office was constructed.

Snowsheds were erected at each end of the tunnel bore to protect the rails. The shed on the Atlantic side was 150 feet in length, and the one on the Pacific side was 650 feet.

Train service through the Alpine Tunnel began in June 1882. The completed project was considered an engineering marvel. At sixteen places on the western descent, walls were laid to provide a shelf for rail construction. The most spectacular shelf is at the Palisades, a mile below the tunnel, where a stone wall 450 feet long, 30 feet high, and 2 feet thick was built from hand-cut stones without mortar. You can see this wall along the drive to the Alpine Tunnel. Over 500,000 feet of California redwood were used to reinforce the tunnel, as workers found loose rock and decomposed granite instead of self-supporting granite. The total cost of the tunnel was more than a quarter of a million dollars.

Many problems plagued the Alpine Tunnel during its period of operation. In March 1884, a train whistle caused a severe snowslide that swept away the town of Woodstock and killed thirteen of its residents. The town was not rebuilt. In 1906, a fire destroyed the wood buildings at Alpine Station; even the stone buildings were demolished when they collapsed from the intense heat of the blaze. In 1910, several people lost their lives when the tunnel caved in. The tunnel was never reopened. Rails were first removed in November 1918; however, the rails in the tunnel itself remain in place. Eventually the railroad property was sold.

Description

This historic route is an easy 2WD road that is popular with tourists and has plenty of pull-offs to enable passing where the road is narrow. The only concern is that it has very steep drop-offs in some sections.

This route starts at the town site of Quartz, approximately three miles northeast of Pitkin on Cumberland Pass Road (FR 765) at the Alpine Tunnel Road turnoff (FR 839). The town was originally founded in 1879 as a mining camp, but it was the arrival of the Denver, South Park & Pacific Railroad in 1882 that spurred its development. It was a major service depot for the railroad.

The remnants of the Midway water tank lie nearly three miles along the route. The tank was so named because it is at the halfway point between Pitkin and the Alpine Tunnel. The tank, which collapsed and has been removed from the base structure, used to hold 47,500 gallons.

A little more than two miles further is the Tunnel Gulch water tank, which has been restored by the Mile High Jeep Club. This 30,000-gallon tank replaced the Woodstock tank. The route continues past the town site of Woodstock. The stone base of the old Woodstock railway water tank is all that remains.

The Sherrod Loop is marked by an information board. The loop was a horseshoe section of track that enabled the trains to turn 228 degrees to remain on the sunnier, south side of the valley. The snow on the north slope was ten to twenty feet deep and typically did not melt until the summer.

About one-and-one-quarter miles after the turnoff to Hancock Pass, you drive across the Palisades, which clings to the cliff face.

The route finishes at a parking area, a short walk from Alpine Station. The telegraph station has been restored, and you can see the ruins of the stone engine house and section house. Volunteers have reconstructed the station platform and relaid 120 feet of the original Denver, South Park & Pacific

RAILROAD WATER TANKS

Depending on the grade and the load, water tanks were typically required at intervals of about thirty miles along a railroad line. They were used to replenish the water carried by the tender—the small car immediately behind the locomotive. The tenders carried coal and about 2,200 gallons of water.

Because of the steep mountain grades between Quartz and the Alpine Tunnel, three tanks were positioned along the tracks. These were originally located at Midway, Woodstock, and Alpine Station.

Tanks were positioned below streams or springs and were gravity-fed. The tank's spout, hinged at the base and upright in its resting position, was lowered onto the tender, and a "flap valve" was opened to fill the tender's tank. The whole operation took about five minutes.

rails. A further short walk takes you to the tunnel entrance, which is completely blocked by a rockslide.

Current Road Conditions

Gunnison National Forest
Gunnison Ranger District
216 North Colorado
Gunnison, CO 81230
(970) 641-0471

Map References

USFS   Gunnison NF
USGS   Chaffee County #2
          Chaffee County #3
          Gunnison County #5
Trails Illustrated, #130
The Roads of Colorado, p. 102
Colorado Atlas & Gazetteer, p. 59

Route Directions

▼ 0.0   From the T-intersection of Alpine Tunnel Road (FR 839) and South-Central #7: Cumberland Pass Trail (FR 765) at the site of Quartz, zero trip meter and pro-

SC Trail #8: Alpine Tunnel Road

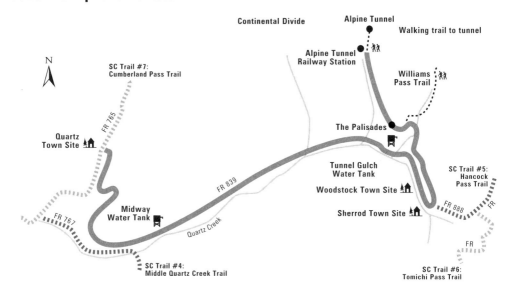

ceed east toward the Alpine Tunnel.

7.3 ▲ End at intersection with South-Central #7: Cumberland Pass Trail.
GPS: N 38°37.47' W 106°28.52'

▼ 3.2 SO Remains of Midway water tank on left. Only base is left standing.

4.1 ▲ SO Remains of Midway water tank on right.

▼ 6.4 SO Tunnel Gulch water tank on left.

0.9 ▲ SO Tunnel Gulch water tank on right.

▼ 7.0 SO Town site of Woodstock on right.

0.3 ▲ SO Town site of Woodstock on left.

▼ 7.2 SO Town site of Sherrod and Sherrod Loop on right.

0.1 ▲ SO Town site of Sherrod and Sherrod Loop on left.

▼ 7.3 TL Intersection with FR 888 (South-Central #5: Hancock Pass Trail). Zero trip meter.

0.0 ▲ At intersection of FR 888 (South-Central #5: Hancock Pass Trail) with FR 839 (Alpine Tunnel Road) zero trip meter and proceed toward Quartz and Pitkin on FR 839.
GPS: N 38°36.83' W 106°23.36'

▼ 0.0 Continue on FR 839 toward Alpine Station.

▼ 0.1 SO South Park Railroad marker on right and Gunnison National Forest.

▼ 0.2 SO Track on left to private cabin.

▼ 0.9 SO Williams Pass Road sign on right.

▼ 1.3 SO Palisades marker on left. Elevation 11,300 feet.

▼ 2.2 Public toilets, picnic tables and gate. It is a short walk to the Alpine Station buildings beyond the gate.
GPS: N 38°38.29' W 106°24.45'

Tincup Pass Trail

STARTING POINT St. Elmo
FINISHING POINT Tincup
TOTAL MILEAGE 12.4 miles
UNPAVED MILEAGE 12.4 miles
DRIVING TIME 1 1/4 hours
ROUTE ELEVATION 12,154 to 9,980 feet
USUALLY OPEN Early July to October
DIFFICULTY RATING 3
SCENIC RATING 8

Special Attractions

- The historic and attractive towns of St. Elmo and Tincup.
- Very attractive scenery, including the summit views and Mirror Lake.
- Access to a network of 4WD trails.
- Excellent backcountry campsites.

History

Tincup Pass was first used by the Indians and then as a pack trail. A wagon road was built following the flood of silver prospectors into the area in 1879. By 1880, the pass was an established freight route, with wagon service run by Witowski and Dunbar's Hack Line. In 1881, it was developed further and became a toll road; soon, three stage lines were running daily stages over the pass. The route was surveyed for a number of railroads, and a tunnel was even started under the pass; but the project was soon abandoned. The pass road was used during World War I to train the cavalry. In 1954, prison laborers upgraded the road.

Tincup was established after the Gold Cup Mine was discovered in 1879, the town was first named Virginia City but its name was changed in 1882. People flooded into Tincup, which in its heyday became the second largest town in Gunnison County. It was notorious as one of the wildest and roughest mining camps in Colorado. Its saloons and gambling parlors operated night and day. Drunkenness and shootings were casual occurrences.

Tincup was ruled by the underworld with organized crime in control of all city offices, many saloons, gaming halls, and the brothels, which seemed to flourish in the early mining camps. When the first marshal started work in 1880, he was told to see nothing, do nothing, and hear nothing; his first arrest would be his last. He lasted only a few months; when he was not paid, he quit. The second marshal occasionally rounded up a few drunks, put them in jail, and then released them. The third marshal decided to harass a saloon owner one night and didn't live long enough to regret it. The fourth marshal went insane and killed him-

Mirror Lake

SC Trail #9: Tincup Pass Trail

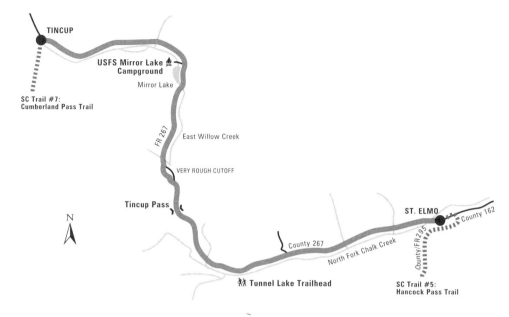

self. The fifth marshal was shot and killed.

Tincup managed to survive through the silver crash of 1893 with its gold and silver production. The town continued into the twentieth century only to end dramatically in a fire that burned it to the ground in 1906. The fire started in a store that sold kerosene. As the flames spread, they destroyed everything in one city block. The town was rebuilt, but it never fully recovered. In 1913, a second fire severely damaged several other buildings.

After the Gold Cup Mine closed in 1917, Tincup declined rapidly and in 1918 the post office closed.

Description

The route starts from the western edge of St. Elmo, a famous ghost town that looks as if it were created by Hollywood, and immediately starts the climb toward the pass. Initially, the road follows the North Fork of Chalk Creek, passing numerous backcountry campsites.

The road is reasonably wide but quite rough, although the surface is sound. As the road progresses, it becomes rockier; but the rocks are imbedded, so the surface remains solid. The road travels through pine and spruce forest.

The summit offers beautiful views of the Arkansas River Valley and the Taylor Park area. Mirror Lake can be glimpsed in the foreground as you look west toward Tincup.

About three miles west of the summit, the road travels along the edge of Mirror Lake, a popular fishing spot. Nearby, there is a U.S.

Tincup Town Hall built in 1906

Forest Service campground. There are also numerous very good backcountry campsites between Mirror Lake and Tincup.

From Mirror Lake, the road is easily negotiated by a car.

Current Road Conditions
Gunnison National Forest
Gunnison Ranger District
216 North Colorado
Gunnison, CO 81230
(970) 641-0471

Map References
USFS   San Isabel NF or Gunnison NF
USGS   Chaffee County #2
         Gunnison County #5
         Gunnison County #3
Trails Illustrated, #129, #130
The Roads of Colorado, p. 101
Colorado Atlas & Gazetteer, p. 59

Route Directions

▼ 0.0   In front of the Miner's Exchange in St. Elmo, zero trip meter and proceed west.
9.3   End in front of the Miner's Exchange in St. Elmo.
      GPS: N 38°42.23′ W 106°20.65′

▼ 0.1   TR   At Tincup sign; then cross bridge over North Fork of Chalk Creek.
9.2 ▲   TL   Onto St. Elmo's main street.

▼ 0.2   BR   Fork in road.
9.1 ▲   BL   Track on right.

▼ 0.4   SO   Poplar Gulch Trailhead on right.
8.9 ▲   SO   Poplar Gulch Trailhead on left.

▼ 0.8   SO   Cattle guard.
8.5 ▲   SO   Cattle guard.

▼ 1.8   SO   Cross over creek.
7.5 ▲   SO   Cross over creek.

▼ 3.0   SO   Track on right.
6.3 ▲   SO   Track on left.

▼ 3.9   SO   Tunnel Lake walking trail on left.
5.4 ▲   SO   Tunnel Lake walking trail on right.
      GPS: N 38°41.54′ W 106°24.80′

▼ 4.6   SO   Cross through creek.
4.7 ▲   SO   Cross through creek.

▼ 6.1   SO   Tincup Pass summit. Enter Gunnison National Forest.
3.2 ▲   SO   Tincup Pass summit. Enter San Isabel National Forest.
      GPS: N 38°42.57′ W 106°26.00′

▼ 6.1   SO   Cattle guard.
3.2 ▲   SO   Cattle guard.

▼ 6.7   BL   Old alternative route is straight ahead.
2.6 ▲   BR   More difficult alternative route rejoins on left.

▼ 7.5   SO   More difficult alternative route rejoins on right.
1.8 ▲   BR   More difficult alternate route on left.

▼ 8.8   SO   Cross through creek at head of Mirror Lake.
0.5 ▲   SO   Cross through creek at head of Mirror Lake.

▼ 9.3   SO   Tincup side of Mirror Lake and angler parking on left. Zero trip meter.
0.0 ▲   BL   Follow track around the left side of Mirror Lake toward Tincup Pass.
      GPS: N 38°44.78′ W 106°25.81′

▼ 0.0   Proceed along Mirror Lake Road (FR 267).
3.1 ▲   BL   Mirror Lake and angler parking on right. Zero trip meter.

▼ 0.1   SO   Track to USFS Mirror Lake Campground on left.
3.0 ▲   SO   Track to USFS Mirror Lake Campground on right.

▼ 0.4   SO   Timberline Trailhead on right.
2.7 ▲   SO   Timberline Trailhead on left.

▼ 0.9   SO   Cross over East Willow Creek.
2.2 ▲   SO   Cross over East Willow Creek.

| ▼ 2.9 | BL | Fork in road. Entering Tincup. |
| 0.2 ▲ | BR | Leaving Tincup. |

| ▼ 3.1 | | End in Tincup at intersection with Cumberland Pass Road (FR 765). |
| 0.0 ▲ | | At intersection of Mirror Lake Road (FR 267) and Cumberland Pass Road (FR 765) in Tincup, zero trip meter and proceed toward Mirror Lake. |

GPS: N 38°45.27' W 106°28.77'

SOUTH-CENTRAL REGION TRAIL #10

Mount Antero Trail

STARTING POINT Intersection of County 162 and Baldwin Creek Road (FR 277)
FINISHING POINT Mount Antero
TOTAL MILEAGE Approximately 6.5 miles
UNPAVED MILEAGE Approximately 6.5 miles
DRIVING TIME 1 3/4 hours (one-way)
ROUTE ELEVATION 14,269 to 9,400 feet
USUALLY OPEN Mid-June to late September
DIFFICULTY RATING 5
SCENIC RATING 9

Special Attractions
- A very challenging and famous 4WD trail.
- Wonderful alpine scenery.
- Access to a network of 4WD trails.

History

Mount Antero is named for Chief "Graceful Walker" Antero of the Uintah band of the Ute Indians. Antero was one of the signatories to the Washington Treaty of 1880, which revised the terms of the Brunot Treaty signed seven years earlier and led to the Ute losing nearly all their land. Antero was a force for peace during the period of very problematic relations between the Ute and the whites in the late 1860s and 1870s. In 1869, John Wesley Powell spent the winter with Antero and Chief Douglas (who was later held responsible for the Meeker Massacre) and learned to speak the Ute language.

While Mount Antero was doubtless examined by prospectors in the late 1870s as silver was being discovered all around, it proved to have little silver to offer. In fact, not a single claim was staked. What the prospectors did not notice, or failed to appreciate, was that Mount Antero offered a fortune in gemstones.

In 1884, a prospector named Nathaniel D. Wanemaker discovered a number of blue aquamarines in the area. He constructed a small stone cabin high on the south side of the mountain. It is said that he discovered six hundred dollars' worth of gems in his first summer and continued to prospect for gems for many years.

Mount Antero has proved extraordinarily rich in aquamarines, topaz, and clear and smoky quartz crystals. The aquamarines range

The switchbacks on the west side of Mount Antero

The network of trails as you climb Mount Antero

in color from pale blue-green to deep blue. Some of the clear crystals from Mount Antero are huge; a seven-inch specimen is on display at the Harvard Mineralogical Museum and another was cut into a six-inch-diameter sphere and displayed at the 1893 Colombian Exposition. The more common smoky quartz crystals weigh as much as fifty pounds.

The most recent mining on Mount Antero has been for beryllium, a lightweight, corrosion-resistant, rigid, steel-gray metallic element that melts only at extremely high temperatures. Beryllium is prized as an aerospace structural material, as a moderator and reflector in nuclear reactors, and in a copper alloy used for springs, electrical contacts, and non-sparking tools. In the 1950s, the access road on the mountain's south shoulder was constructed by the company mining the beryllium.

Description

The Mount Antero route starts at the intersection of the road between Nathrop and St. Elmo (County 162) and FR 277. The turnoff is 12 miles west of US 285 along County 162 and 3.3 miles east of St. Elmo.

FR 277 ascends steeply right from the point of departure from County 162. It is a rough, rocky shelf road through the pine and aspen forest but offers some very good views back into the valley and the township of Alpine. The track is narrow and has some very steep drop-offs. Pull-offs for passing other vehicles are only just adequate in some sections. High clearance is definitely required, but if you carefully select your line, the rocks are not large enough to cause vehicle damage.

Some good news: Once you have completed the first two miles, you are past the most difficult section of the route.

At the 2.7-mile point, you cross through Baldwin Creek, which has a firm base and is usually only about a foot deep. From the creek crossing, the road again climbs a couple of loose talus slopes before emerging above timberline. The road then commences a series of narrow switchbacks before winding around the south face and continuing up the east face. Passing opportunities are limited in this section, so it pays to watch for oncoming vehicles and plan ahead.

At the 3.8-mile point, there is an intersection. The track on the right leads to a dead end. This is the last chance to turn around before the end of the road, and the next section is more difficult than anything encountered until this point. (Note: The difficulty rating for this route is based on stopping

SC Trail #10: Mount Antero Trail

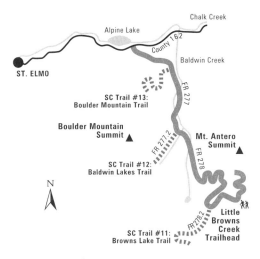

here.) We recommend that if you wish to see the last half mile of the road, you walk it.

Current Road Conditions
San Isabel National Forest
Salida Ranger District
325 West Rainbow Boulevard
Salida, CO 81201
(719) 539-3591

Map References
USFS   San Isabel NF
USGS   Chaffee County #2
        Chaffee County #3
Trails Illustrated, #130
The Roads of Colorado, p. 102
Colorado Atlas & Gazetteer, pp. 59-60

Route Directions

▼ 0.0   From County 162 (3.3 miles east of St. Elmo), turn onto Baldwin Creek Road (FR 277) toward Mt. Antero and zero trip meter.
           GPS: N 38°42.60′ W 106°17.46′

▼ 1.1   SO Track on right is South-Central #13: Boulder Mountain Trail.

▼ 2.7   TL South-Central #12: Baldwin Lakes Trail is straight ahead (FR 277.2). Zero trip meter.
           GPS: N 38°40.99′ W 106°16.32′

▼ 0.0   Cross through Baldwin Creek and continue on FR 278 toward Mt. Antero.

▼ 0.2   SO Cross through creek.

▼ 0.3   SO Track on left.

▼ 1.5   SO Cross through creek.

▼ 3.3   BL South-Central #11: Browns Lake Trail (278.2) on right. Remain on 278.A.
           GPS: N 38°39.70′ W 106°15.43′

▼ 3.4   SO Intersection with 278.B on right, which climbs Mt. White, providing spectacular views all around, especially looking back at Mt. Antero and into the valley to the south.

▼ 3.8   BL Track on right. Park and walk remaining section.
           GPS: N 38°39.74′ W 106°14.94′

SOUTH-CENTRAL REGION TRAIL #11

Browns Lake Trail

STARTING POINT Intersection of South-Central #10: Mount Antero Trail (FR 278A) and FR 278.2
FINISHING POINT Browns Creek Trailhead
TOTAL MILEAGE 3.3 miles
UNPAVED MILEAGE 3.3 miles
DRIVING TIME 3/4 hour (one-way)
ROUTE ELEVATION 12,800 to 11,400 feet
USUALLY OPEN Mid-June to late September
DIFFICULTY RATING 4
SCENIC RATING 10

Special Attractions
- The extremely scenic Browns Lake.
- Part of a network of 4WD trails near the summit of Mount Antero.

Description
The 4WD trail to Browns Lake, a side road from the Mount Antero road, sees much less traffic than that more-famous route.

After turning off the Mount Antero road, you cross an alpine meadow before commencing the rocky descent down into Browns

Browns Lake

Creek Valley. The road enters the timberline and wends its way through the pine forest with rather tight clearance between the trees.

The trail proceeds past the remains of a mining camp, including the ruins of a miner's cabin. As you proceed toward the trailhead and the end of the 4WD road, you'll enjoy picture-postcard views of Browns Lake, located in the valley at an altitude of 11,286 feet.

The road is moderately difficult, with sections of narrow switchbacks, loose surface rock, and some tight clearances; but the solitude and the scenery make it all worthwhile.

Current Road Conditions

San Isabel National Forest
Salida Ranger District
325 West Rainbow Boulevard
Salida, CO 81201
(719) 539-3591

Map References

USFS   San Isabel NF
USGS   Chaffee County #3
Trails Illustrated, #130
The Roads of Colorado, p. 102
Colorado Atlas & Gazetteer, pp. 59-60

The road approaching Browns Lake

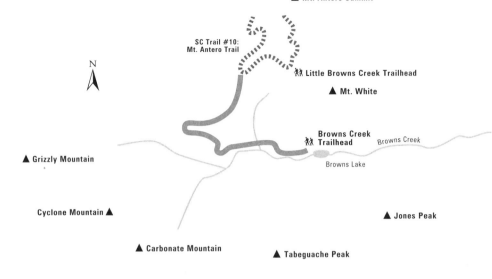

Route Directions

▼ 0.0   At intersection of Mt. Antero Trail (FR 278.A) and trail to Browns Lake (FR 278.2), zero trip meter and proceed along FR 278.2 into the valley.
         GPS: N 38°39.70' W 106°15.43'

▼ 1.9   SO Cabin ruins on right.
▼ 2.0   SO Cabin ruins on left.
▼ 2.5   SO Cross through creek.
▼ 3.3   Track ends at Browns Creek Trailhead.
         GPS: N 38°38.63' W 106°14.70'

SOUTH-CENTRAL REGION TRAIL #12

Baldwin Lakes Trail

STARTING POINT Intersection of South-Central #10: Mount Antero Trail (FR 278) and Baldwin Creek Road (FR 277)
FINISHING POINT Parking area at Baldwin Lakes
TOTAL MILEAGE 2.9 miles
UNPAVED MILEAGE 2.9 miles
DRIVING TIME 1 hour (one-way)
ROUTE ELEVATION 12,200 to 10,880 feet

USUALLY OPEN Mid-June to late September
DIFFICULTY RATING 5
SCENIC RATING 7

Special Attractions

■ Challenging 4WD trail.
■ Scenic views of Baldwin Lakes.

Description

The Baldwin Lakes route is a very rough and rocky side road to the Mount Antero road. The talus roadbed is slippery, and sharp rocks make a flat tire a continual threat.

The first section of road travels along the creek, past open meadows and many backcountry camping spots. As it continues up to the first lake, you travel though the pine forest, emerging to cross huge talus rockslides and then reentering the forest. About two miles along the road, the surface rock becomes mostly imbedded in the soil and more stable. There is a fairly steep section where the melting snow drains across the trail, making it boggy and, somewhat slippery when you are going uphill. The last section of the road has large imbedded rocks to negotiate before you reach the small parking area.

Views of Baldwin Creek Valley, the high

Baldwin Lakes

Route Directions

▼ 0.0   From the intersection of FR 278 and FR 277.2, at the small parking area beside Baldwin Creek crossing, zero trip meter and proceed toward Baldwin Lakes.
GPS: N 38°40.97' W 106°16.34'

▼ 0.2 SO Remains of log cabin.
▼ 0.9 BR Fork in road.
▼ 1.5 BL Fork in road. Follow lower track (FR 277). Track on right goes to old mine farther up the mountain.
GPS: N 38°40.14' W 106°17.45'

▼ 2.2 BR Small parking area on left with view of the lakes and a walking track.
GPS: N 38°39.69' W 106°18.10'

▼ 2.9   Small parking/turn-around area. From this point, the track becomes more difficult than our rating indicates. Large, imbedded rocks make impact with the underside of the vehicle likely.
GPS: N 38°39.95' W 106°18.36'

SC Trail #12: Baldwin Lakes Trail

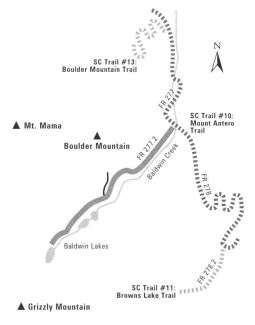

alpine bowl encircled by steep valley walls, and the lakes cradled in its base combine to make the journey very scenic.

Current Road Conditions
San Isabel National Forest
Salida Ranger District
325 West Rainbow Boulevard
Salida, CO 81201
(719) 539-3591

Map References
USFS   San Isabel NF
USGS   Chaffee County #2
        Chaffee County #3 (incomplete)
Trails Illustrated, #130
The Roads of Colorado, p. 102
Colorado Atlas & Gazetteer, p. 59

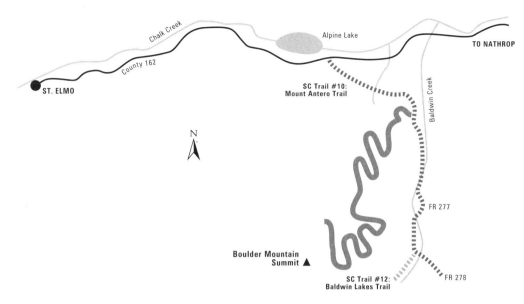

Boulder Mountain Trail

STARTING POINT Intersection of Baldwin Creek Road (FR 277) and Boulder Mountain Road

FINISHING POINT Mine shaft and cabin ruins near the top of the mountain

TOTAL MILEAGE 4.8 miles

UNPAVED MILEAGE 4.8 miles

DRIVING TIME 1 1/4 hours (one-way)

ROUTE ELEVATION 12,800 to 9,950 feet

USUALLY OPEN Mid-June to late September

DIFFICULTY RATING 5

SCENIC RATING 8

Special Attractions

■ Challenging 4WD trail.
■ Spectacular alpine views.

Description

This route, another side road to the Mount Antero Trail, is also rough and rocky but less so than the Mount Antero road. The challenge of this road is that it is narrow with very high drop-offs. To make matters more interesting, especially if you have a full-sized vehicle, small pine trees grow on the inside edge of the track, pushing you perilously close to the edge. To add to the excitement, sections of the road are significantly off-camber!

The road carries less traffic than others in the area, which is fortunate because there are sections where the only way to get around an oncoming vehicle is for one vehicle to reverse a good distance. Remember that the vehicle going uphill has the right of way, but common sense should always prevail. Because of the steep talus slopes, you have to stop often and clear rubble off the road.

On the way up, the route affords some wonderful, panoramic views across to the Mount Antero road and the adjoining mountain peaks; but when you reach the mine at the top, the view is truly spectacular—across the Chalk Creek Valley, Alpine Lake, and the township of Alpine.

At the end of the trail are the windswept ruins of an old mine cabin and an open mine portal set into the bare, talus slope.

Current Road Conditions

San Isabel National Forest
Salida Ranger District
325 West Rainbow Boulevard
Salida, CO 81201
(719) 539-3591

Map References
USFS San Isabel NF
USGS Chaffee County #2
Trails Illustrated, #130
The Roads of Colorado, p. 102
Colorado Atlas & Gazetteer, p. 59

Route Directions

▼ 0.0   From the 1.1-mile mark on Mt. Antero
        Trail (Baldwin Creek Road), zero trip
        meter and make a sharp right turn onto
        an unmarked, rocky, track.
        GPS: N 38°42.21' W 106°16.47'

▼ 0.9   SO   Campsites off to the left and right.
             Then cabin ruins and track on left.
▼ 4.8   Top of track. Mine shaft and ruins.
             GPS: N 38°41.20' W 106°17.32'

A relatively easy section of Boulder Mountain Trail

SOUTH-CENTRAL REGION TRAIL #14

Pomeroy Lakes and Mary Murphy Mine Trail

STARTING POINT Intersection of South-Central
    #5: Hancock Pass Trail (FR 295) and
    FR 297.1
FINISHING POINT Parking area at Pomeroy Lakes
TOTAL MILEAGE 2.7 miles
UNPAVED MILEAGE 2.7 miles
DRIVING TIME 1 hour (one-way)
ROUTE ELEVATION 12,035 to 10,500 feet
USUALLY OPEN Mid-June to late September
DIFFICULTY RATING 5
SCENIC RATING 7

Special Attractions
■ Remains of the Mary Murphy Mine.
■ A varied, challenging, short 4WD trail.
■ Pomeroy Lakes in their barren, scenic, alpine setting.

History
According to legend, Dr. A. E. Wright, who discovered the Mary Murphy Mine in the mid-1870s, named it after a nurse who cared for him when he was taken to the hospital in Denver. If Mary was a nurse with whom Wright was smitten, it is not clear who the adjoining Pat Murphy Mine was named after. One thing is certain: The Mary Murphy Mine was enormously successful and was the main engine of the local economy. It supported the towns of St. Elmo, Romley, and Hancock. When the mine closed in 1926, it spelled the end for these towns and also for the remaining section of the old Alpine Tunnel railroad. The tracks were torn up within the year.

Description
This route starts along the road to Hancock that follows the Alpine Tunnel railroad grade.

MINING

Gold and silver deposits are frequently found together. They are formed when molten minerals are forced up from deep within the earth into the bedrock. Commonly, the host rock is quartz.

Over time, erosion breaks down the rock deposits and the gold is freed and left in pure form. Water then disperses the free gold along streambeds. These free deposits are known as "placers." A deposit of gold that is still contained in a rock formation is called a "lode."

Placer Mining Because placers are relatively easy to find, they are normally the first gold deposits discovered in any area. Miners typically follow the placers upstream to the mother lode.

Placer mining is the simplest form of mining operations, since it merely involves separating the free gold from the dirt, mud, or gravel with which it is mixed. The process takes a number of forms: simple panning; sluicing to process a larger volume, using the same principle as panning; dredging to process even larger volumes of rock; and hydraulic mining, used where the ancient riverbeds had long since disappeared, leaving the gold on dry land. Hydraulic mining uses hoses to bring water from up to three miles distant and wash away the extraneous material to recover the gold.

Placer mining was known as "poor man's mining," because panning a creek could be done with very little capital. Colorado's placer production has been nearly all for gold.

Hard-Rock Mining Hard-rock mining involves digging ore out of the ground and recovering it from the quartz (or other minerals) surrounding it.

Hard-rock mining in its simplest form involves tunneling horizontally under the vein (either directly or from an initial vertical shaft), and then digging out the ore into mine cars placed beneath it. In the 1800s, mining cars were pulled by mules along tracks laid in the mines. If the mine incorporated a vertical shaft, then a hoist would lift the ore to the surface. Digging the shafts was made much easier during the 1870s, when hand-drilling techniques were made obsolete by machine drills and dynamite.

Stamp Mills Once extracted from the mine, the gold had to be separated from the host rock. To do this economically in the latter half of the nineteenth century, mining companies made use of stamp mills. Often tramways had to be built to transport the ore to these large structures that processed the ore in stages. Stamp mills had to be near water and on steep downhill slopes. Milling involved progressively crushing the ore and then processing it chemically to extract the precious metal. Mine workers brought the ore into the mill and fed it into a stamper, which weighed up to a ton. The stamper crushed the host rock; then a slurry of the crushed ore and water was fed over a series of mercury-coated amalgamation plates, which captured the precious metal.

Because hard-rock mining required substantial capital to develop the mine and build the mill, it was usually undertaken by large corporations. The men who worked the mines were employees of the corporations, which explains why labor union problems often occurred in hard-rock mines.

Mary Murphy Mine tram support

Mine ruins

After turning onto FR 297, the road passes many remains of the Mary Murphy Mine, located high above the road on the mountainside. Towers used by the tramway, which extended over two miles into Pomeroy Gulch from the railway grade, are still clearly evident as you drive along the initial section of the road. There are also a number of buildings where the tramway deposited the ore that it carried down from the top of the mountain.

Until this point the road is suitable for 2WD vehicles, but as the route proceeds along FR 297.2, the road becomes high-clearance 4WD only.

Continuing toward the lake, you pass a number of good backcountry camping sites and a grave on the side of the road that dates back to 1884.

The road gets progressively rockier and more rutted and eroded before reaching the parking area near the lakes, merely 2.7 miles from the start.

Current Road Conditions

San Isabel National Forest
Salida Ranger District
325 West Rainbow Boulevard
Salida, CO 81201
(719) 539-3591

Map References

USFS   San Isabel NF
USGS   Chaffee County #2
       Chaffee County #3
Trails Illustrated, #130
The Roads of Colorado, p. 102
Colorado Atlas & Gazetteer, p. 59

Route Directions

▼ 0.0   At the intersection of South-Central #5: Hancock Pass Trail (FR 295) with sign to Mary Murphy Mine and Pomeroy Lakes, zero trip meter and proceed along FR 297.1.
         GPS: N 38°40.38' W 106°21.95'

SC Trail #14: Pomeroy Lakes and Mary Murphy Mine Trail

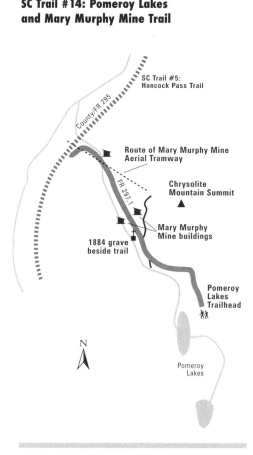

SC Trail #5:
Hancock Pass Trail

County/FR 295

Route of Mary Murphy Mine
Aerial Tramway

FR 297.1

Chrysolite
Mountain Summit
▲

Mary Murphy
Mine buildings

1884 grave
beside trail

Pomeroy
Lakes
Trailhead

N

Pomeroy
Lakes

▼ 0.2   SO   Rocky ascent. Mine ruins on right.
▼ 0.3   SO   Cabin on left. Cross over creek.
▼ 0.6   SO   Track on left.
▼ 0.7   SO   Mary Murphy Mine headquarters on right. Mine and tailing on left.
▼ 0.8   SO   Tracks on left.
▼ 0.9   SO   Gated track on left goes to Mary Murphy Mine ruins. Zero trip meter.
             GPS: N 38°39.95' W 106°21.34'

▼ 0.0   BR   Continue on FR 297.2 to Pomeroy Lakes.
▼ 0.2   SO   Track on right.
▼ 0.5   SO   Short track on left to mine ruins up the hill. Cross through creek.
▼ 0.7   SO   Grave on right (date: 1857-1884).
▼ 0.8   SO   Track on left.
▼ 1.0   TL   Track on right and straight ahead to campsites.

▼ 1.2   SO   Cross through creek.
▼ 1.8   End at Pomeroy Lakes and parking area.
             GPS: N 38°38.90' W 106°20.34'

Marshall Pass Poncha Creek Trail

STARTING POINT Mears Junction at US 285 and FR 200, 5 miles south of Poncha Springs
FINISHING POINT Marshall Pass
TOTAL MILEAGE 11.2 miles
UNPAVED MILEAGE 11.2 miles
DRIVING TIME 1 1/4 hours
ROUTE ELEVATION 10,846 to 8,595 feet
USUALLY OPEN Mid-June to late September
DIFFICULTY RATING 3
SCENIC RATING 8

Special Attractions

■ 4WD alternative to the railroad grade route to Marshall Pass.
■ Very good views, especially as the summit is approached.
■ Access to good backcountry campsites, fishing, and many hiking trails.

Description

This route is narrower, rougher, and scenically more varied than the main road to Marshall Pass, which follows the old railroad grade (South-Central #16). However, while not suitable for passenger vehicles, it offers little difficulty to a 4WD vehicle.

The trail starts at Mears Junction, which is the intersection of US 285 and County/FR 200. This was the junction of two of Otto Mears's toll roads and is about 5 miles south of Poncha Springs and 2.4 miles north of Poncha Pass.

From the turnoff onto FR 203, the track gets progressively narrower and rougher, although it remains suitable for passenger vehicles in dry conditions. After Starvation

Creek, creek crossings and the rougher road make a high-clearance vehicle necessary.

FR 203 offers numerous undeveloped campsites beside Poncha Creek for the first six miles after its intersection with County/FR 200. From this point, the trail starts its ascent toward the pass, and camping possibilities become scarce. Eventually, the road departs from the creek to make the final climb through a series of alpine meadows, offering spectacular views before reaching the pass.

There are some very good backcountry campsites and numerous fishing spots beside Poncha Creek. For those who prefer more of the comforts of home, the particularly scenic O'Haver Lake offers a developed U.S. Forest Service campground with access for RVs and camper trailers. A number of hiking trails run through the area, including the Colorado Trail and the Continental Divide Trail.

Old railway bridge over Poncha Creek

Current Road Conditions
San Isabel National Forest
Salida Ranger District
325 West Rainbow Boulevard
Salida, CO 81201
(719) 539-3591

Map References
USFS   Gunnison NF
      San Isabel NF
USGS   Chaffee County #3
      Saguache County #2
Trails Illustrated, #139
The Roads of Colorado, p. 102
Colorado Atlas & Gazetteer, pp. 69-70

Route Directions

▼ 0.0   At Mears Junction, zero trip meter and turn from US 285 onto County/FR 200 and proceed west across cattle guard.

11.2 ▲   Cross cattle guard and end at intersection with US 285.

      GPS: N 38°26.89' W 106°06.40'

▼ 1.8 SO Railway bridge ruins on left.
9.4 ▲ SO Railway bridge ruins on right.

▼ 2.2 TR Shirley town site on left. Turn onto FR 202.
9.0 ▲ TL Onto County 200.

▼ 2.6 SO Camping on right and left.
8.6 ▲ SO Camping on right and left.

▼ 3.1 TL Toward Poncha Creek on FR 200. O'Haver Lake is 0.5 miles straight ahead on FR 202, with fishing access and developed camping. South-Central #16: Marshall Pass Railroad Grade Road (FR 200) is to the right.
8.1 ▲ TR Onto FR 202.
      GPS: N 38°25.37' W 106°08.45'

▼ 3.9 SO Track on right. Beaver Creek sign.
7.3 ▲ SO Track on left. Beaver Creek sign.

▼ 4.1 BR Signpost reads "Via Poncha Creek 7– FR 203." Intersection. Numerous good backcountry camping spots are found all along Poncha Creek.
7.1 ▲ BL Intersection.
      GPS: N 38°24.92' W 106°08.31'

▼ 6.5 SO Trailhead for Starvation Creek walking trail.
4.7 ▲ SO Trailhead for Starvation Creek walking trail.

▼ 6.7 SO Track on right is 0.25 miles in length with additional camping spots.

4.5 ▲ SO Track on left.

▼ 7.7 SO Cross over Tent Creek.

3.5 ▲ SO Cross over Tent Creek.

▼ 8.2 SO Track on left down to Poncha Creek and numerous campsites down below the road.

3.0 ▲ SO Track on right.

▼ 8.6 SO Cross over creek. Slightly further, there's a short track on the right and four campsites.

2.6 ▲ SO Track on left, then cross over creek.
GPS: N 38°23.70' W106°12.50

▼ 9.9 SO Cross over Ouray Creek.

1.3 ▲ SO Cross over Ouray Creek.

▼ 10.0 SO Camping on right and left in grassy areas; then cross through Poncha Creek.

1.2 ▲ SO Cross through Poncha Creek.

▼ 10.1 SO Open meadow on left with scenic views of valley and Sangre de Cristo mountain range to the east. No vehicle access.

1.1 ▲ SO Open meadow on right with scenic views.

▼ 10.2 SO Track on left to campsite.

.1.0 ▲ SO Track on right to campsite.

▼ 10.6 SO 4WD track on left (203.1A) to Starvation Creek walking trail. This side trip leads 1.6 miles to TR 1408, which loops back to Marshall Pass after 6.6 miles. At the 1.8 mile point there is a scenic overlook. GPS: N 38°22.96' W 106°13.19'.

0.6 ▲ SO Track on right to scenic overlooks.
GPS: N 38°23.53' W 106°14.22'

▼ 11.1 TL Intersection with South-Central #16: Marshall Pass Railroad Grade Road (FR 200). Track on left is the Colorado Trail.

0.1 ▲ TR FR 200 continues straight ahead.
GPS: N 38°23.50' W 106°14.75'

▼ 11.2 Summit of Marshall Pass. Zero trip meter. South-Central #17: Marshall Pass to Sargents continues to Sargents.

0.0 ▲ Summit of Marshall Pass. Zero trip meter.
GPS: N 38°23.50' W 106°14.85'

SC Trail #15: Marshall Pass Poncha Creek Trail

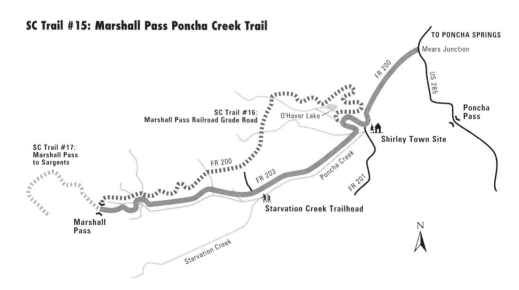

Marshall Pass summit

Marshall Pass Railway Grade Road

STARTING POINT Mears Junction at US 285 and FR 200, 5 miles south of Poncha Springs
FINISHING POINT Marshall Pass
TOTAL MILEAGE 13.4
UNPAVED MILEAGE 13.4
DRIVING TIME 1/2 hour
ROUTE ELEVATION 10,842 to 8,595 feet
USUALLY OPEN Late May to mid-October
DIFFICULTY RATING 1
SCENIC RATING 7

Special Attractions
■ Easy, scenic road along a historic railroad grade.
■ Developed campground and good fishing at picturesque O'Haver Lake.
■ Provides a loop route between Marshall Pass and Mears Junction, when combined with South-Central #15: Marshall Pass Poncha Creek Trail.

History
This pass is named for Lieutenant William L. Marshall, who discovered it while on the Wheeler survey expedition in 1873.

Reportedly, he was suffering from a toothache and sought a quicker route back to Denver and relief from a dentist!

In 1877, Otto Mears constructed a wagon road to Gunnison across the pass from his Poncha Pass toll road. It served as a stagecoach route until the opening of the railroad and was used by President Grant in 1880. Mears sold the road to the Denver & Rio Grande Railroad. The Denver & Rio Grande was embroiled in a classic railroad battle during the early 1880s in its race to be first to link the Arkansas Valley and the Gunnison Basin area. The Denver, South Park & Pacific Railroad chose a route that necessitated the construction of the famous Alpine Tunnel (South-Central #8).

Denver & Rio Grande train climbing the grade to Marshall Pass in 1900

SC Trail #16: Marshall Pass Railroad Grade Road

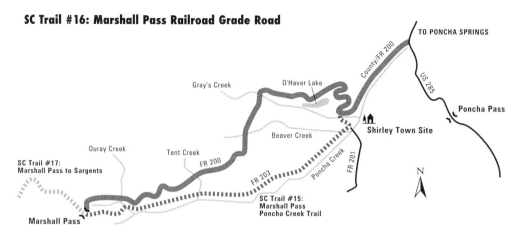

With the aid of twenty-three snowsheds to protect it from the elements, a Denver & Rio Grande narrow-gauge railway won the battle by using the Marshall Pass route. Operations commenced in 1881 and continued until 1953. The tracks were dismantled in 1955. A post office, located at the station at the top of the pass, continued to operate until 1952. President William H. Taft was probably the most famous passenger to cross the pass by train.

Description

This route follows the old railroad grade and is easier than the alternative route via Poncha Creek (South-Central #15). The route is unpaved but wide and well graded. It is suitable for RVs and trailers making their way to the campground at O'Haver Lake or across Marshall Pass on County 200.

The trail starts at Mears Junction, which is the intersection of US 285 and County/FR 200. Once the junction of two of Otto Mears's toll roads, the intersection is located about 5 miles south of Poncha Springs and 2.4 miles north of Poncha Pass.

O'Haver Lake offers good fishing and a developed U.S. Forest Service campground with access for RVs and camper trailers. A number of hiking trails run through the area, including the Colorado Trail and the Continental Divide Trail.

Current Road Conditions

San Isabel National Forest
Salida Ranger District
325 West Rainbow Boulevard
Salida, CO 81201
(719) 539-3591

Map References

USFS   Gunnison NF
       San Isabel NF
USGS   Chaffee County #3
       Saguache County #2
Trails Illustrated, #139
The Roads of Colorado, p. 102
Colorado Atlas & Gazetteer, pp. 69-70

Route Directions

▼ 0.0   At Mears Junction zero trip meter and turn from US 285 onto County/FR 200 heading west across cattle guard.

13.4 ▲   Cross cattle guard and end at intersection with US 285.

GPS: N 38°26.89' W 106°06.40'

▼ 2.2 TR Shirley town site. Public toilets on left. Turn right onto FR 202.

11.2 ▲ TL Turn left onto County/FR 200. Shirley town site and public toilets on right.

▼ 3.1 TR Intersection with County/FR 200. O'Haver Lake is straight ahead, with fishing access and developed camping.

South-Central #15: Marshall Pass Poncha Creek Trail is to the left.

10.3 ▲ TL Intersection with FR 202. O'Haver Lake is to the right. South-Central #15: Marshall Pass Poncha Creek Trail is straight ahead.

GPS: N 38°25.37′ W 106°08.45′

▼ 4.8 SO Seasonal closure gate. Track on right is County 204.

8.6 ▲ SO Track on left is County 204. Seasonal closure gate.

▼ 5.5 SO O'Haver Lake on left below road.

7.9 ▲ SO O'Haver Lake on right below road.

▼ 7.0 SO Cross over Gray's Creek.

6.4 ▲ SO Cross over Gray's Creek.

▼ 9.9 SO Cross over Tent Creek.

3.5 ▲ SO Cross over Tent Creek.

▼ 10.3 SO Track on right.

3.1 ▲ SO Track on left.

▼ 12.1 SO Old railway embankment across Ouray Creek.

1.3 ▲ SO Old railway embankment across Ouray Creek.

▼ 13.0 SO Hiking trail on right to South Fooses Creek and Monarch Pass.

0.4 ▲ SO Hiking trail on left to South Fooses Creek and Monarch Pass.

▼ 13.1 SO Marshall Pass Trailhead sign and public toilets on left.

0.3 ▲ SO Marshall Pass Trailhead sign and public toilets on right.

▼ 13.3 SO Road on left is South-Central #15: Marshall Pass Poncha Creek Trail. Track on left is the Colorado Trail.

0.1 ▲ BL Track on right is the Colorado Trail. Then South-Central #15: Marshall Pass Poncha Creek Trail is on right.

▼ 13.4 Summit of Marshall Pass. Zero trip

meter. South-Central #17: Marshall Pass to Sargents continues to Sargents.

0.0 ▲ Marshall Pass summit. Zero trip meter.

GPS: N 38°23.50′ W 106°14.85′

Marshall Pass to Sargents

STARTING POINT Marshall Pass
FINISHING POINT Sargents
TOTAL MILEAGE 16.3 miles
UNPAVED MILEAGE 16.3 miles
DRIVING TIME 3/4 hour
ROUTE ELEVATION 10,846 to 8,420 feet
USUALLY OPEN Late May to late October
DIFFICULTY RATING 1
SCENIC RATING 5

Special Attractions
■ Northern access to Marshall Pass.
■ Steamtrain water tank in Sargents.

History
The two routes between Mears Junction and Marshall Pass join at the summit. FR 243 continues along the old railway grade built by the Denver & Rio Grande Railroad in 1881.

Sargents was established in the late 1870s and was named for Joseph Sargent who had been employed at the Los Piños Indian Agency and had established a ranch in the area in 1879. Initially the settlement was known as Marshalltown but the name was changed in 1882. The town never grew very large and in the late 1880s had a population of only about 150.

Description
This journey runs through gentle, rolling countryside and ranch land with many stands of aspens adding color in the fall. At Sargents, there is an old wooden water tank that used to service the steam locomotives that chugged up Marshall Pass from 1881 to 1953.

Current Road Conditions

San Isabel National Forest
Salida Ranger District
325 West Rainbow Boulevard
Salida, CO 81201
(719) 539-3591

Map References

USFS Gunnison NF
       San Isabel NF
USGS Saguache County #1
       Saguache County #2
Trails Illustrated, #139
The Roads of Colorado, p. 102
Colorado Atlas & Gazetteer, p. 69

Route Directions

▼ 0.0   SO From the summit of Marshall Pass, zero trip meter and proceed west across cattle guard. FR 243 sign. Track on right.

16.3 ▲ SO Track on left; then San Isabel National Forest sign and cattle guard. Summit of Marshall Pass. (To continue, refer to South-Central #15 or #16.)
      GPS: N 38°23.50' W 106°14.85'

Old railroad tank at Sargents

▼ 0.1   SO Seasonal gate.
16.2 ▲ SO Seasonal gate.

▼ 0.9   SO Track on left.
15.4 ▲ SO Track on right.

▼ 1.2   SO Track on left.
15.1 ▲ SO Track on right.

▼ 3.8   SO Track on left for hiking, horses, and snowmobiles.
12.5 ▲ SO Track on right for non-motorized vehicles.

▼ 4.2   SO Cattle guard.
12.0 ▲ SO Cattle guard.

▼ 5.9   SO Cross Millswitch Creek. Two tracks (closed) on left.
10.4 ▲ SO Two tracks (closed) on right. Cross Millswitch Creek.

▼ 8.1   SO Track on right to site of Chester
8.1 ▲ SO Track on left to site of Chester.
      GPS: N 38°22.28' W 106°18.45'

▼ 10.9 TL Seasonal gate. Intersection with road on right.
5.4 ▲ TR Intersection and seasonal gate. Take FR 243 toward Marshall Pass.
      GPS: N 38°22.20' W 106°20.62'

▼ 11.4 SO Cattle guard.
4.9 ▲ SO Cattle guard. Entering National Forest sign.

▼ 11.9 SO Sign: "Indian Creek." Road on right is County 35 W. (You are on County XX 32.)
4.4 ▲ SO County 35 W on left goes to a network of 4WD tracks and the Pinnacle Mine.

▼ 16.3 SO End at intersection with US 50 in Sargents.
0.0 ▲   At intersection of US 50 and County XX 32 (FR 243) in Sargents, zero trip meter and proceed along the county road toward Marshall Pass.
      GPS: N 38°24.46' W 106°24.90'

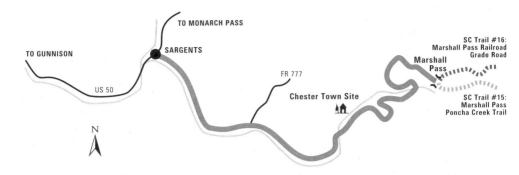

SOUTH-CENTRAL REGION TRAIL #18

Cochetopa Pass Road

STARTING POINT Saguache Junction at the intersection of US 285 and Colorado 114

FINISHING POINT Los Piños Pass Road at the intersection of NN 14 and 15 GG

TOTAL MILEAGE 39.6 miles

UNPAVED MILEAGE 18.9 miles

DRIVING TIME 1 1/4 hours

ROUTE ELEVATION 10,032 to 7,800 feet

USUALLY OPEN Always open

DIFFICULTY RATING 1

SCENIC RATING 5

Special Attractions

■ Easy, historic pass road.
■ Access to a network of 4WD trails.

History

"Cochetopa" is the Ute word for "pass or gate of the buffalo." The Utes used the pass for centuries before the first documented crossing by the Spanish in 1779. It was frequently used by traders, trappers, and early explorers before the days of white settlement.

Cochetopa Pass's relatively gentle grades made it suitable for wagons; the first vehicles to cross the Continental Divide in Colorado were the wagons of Antoine Robidoux in 1825. Subsequently, parties exploring the area frequently used the pass. The easy grades in the area allowed for a variety of routes across the Divide. In 1853, the expeditions of Frémont, Gunnison, and Beale each traveled a different route. Use of the pass increased as miners and settlers moved through the area.

John Lawrence built a road over the pass in 1869, and from that time, the route carried a regular stagecoach mail run. Otto Mears further improved it as a toll road in 1875, providing access to Silverton and Gunnison from his Poncha Pass toll road.

Description

The pass road remains an easy journey on a well-maintained road. The east side of the pass offers better scenery, with a varied environment of rock formations, pine forest, and open fields. On the west side of the pass, there is a broad view across Cochetopa Park to the rugged San Juan Mountains rising above Lake City.

This area has an extensive network of side roads (including South-Central #19) that covers a large expanse of national forest, offering the curious four-wheel driver plenty of exploring along little-used tracks through mainly gentle, rolling countryside.

Current Road Conditions

Gunnison National Forest
Gunnison Ranger District
216 North Colorado
Gunnison, CO 81230
(970) 641-0471

Map References

USFS   Rio Grande NF
        Gunnison NF

A section of trail along Cochetopa Pass Road

USGS Saguache County #1
Trails Illustrated, #139
The Roads of Colorado, p. 117
Colorado Atlas & Gazetteer, pp. 69-70

Route Directions

▼ 0.0   From Saguache, at the junction of US 285 and Colorado 114, zero trip meter and proceed west on Colorado 114.

20.7 ▲   End at intersection of US 285 and Colorado 114.

      GPS: N 38°05.33' W 106°08.50'

▼ 1.2   SO   Ute Pass turnoff on right.

19.5 ▲   SO   Ute Pass turnoff on left.

▼ 10.4   SO   Stay on Colorado 114. Sargents turnoff on right.

10.3 ▲   SO   Road to Sargents on left.

▼ 20.0   SO   Squaw Creek (30 CC) sign on left.

0.7 ▲   SO   Squaw Creek (30 CC) sign on right.

▼ 20.7   TL   Turn onto County NN 14. Signs to Luders Creek CG, Cochetopa Pass, and Dome Lakes. Zero trip meter.

0.0 ▲   Continue toward Saguache.

      GPS: N 38°07.94' W 106°27.73'

▼ 0.0   Continue straight ahead on NN 14 toward Cochetopa Pass.

5.4 ▲   TR   Turn onto Colorado 114. Paved.

▼ 1.6   SO   Cattle guard. Travel through Rabbit Canyon.

3.8 ▲   SO   Cattle guard. Travel through Rabbit Canyon.

▼ 5.4   BL   South-Central #19: Taylor Canyon Trail (FR 768) on right. Zero trip meter.

0.0 ▲   Proceed straight ahead on NN-14.

      GPS: N 38°09.55' W 106°32.70'

▼ 0.0   Proceed straight ahead on NN 14 toward Cochetopa Pass.

4.8 ▲   BR   South-Central #19: Taylor Canyon Trail (FR 768) on left. Zero trip meter.

▼ 0.6   TR   Intersection with FR 740 to Windy Point.

4.2 ▲   TL   Intersection with FR 740 to Windy Point.

▼ 2.9	SO	Alternative way to Taylor Canyon on right.
1.9 ▲	SO	Alternative way to Taylor Canyon on left.

▼ 3.0	SO	Luders Creek Campground on right.
1.8 ▲	SO	Luders Creek Campground on left.

▼ 4.4	SO	Firewood collection area on left.
0.4 ▲	SO	Firewood collection area on right.

▼ 4.8	SO	Track on left. Cattle guard. Then Cochetopa Pass marker. Zero trip meter.
0.0 ▲		Continue along track.
		GPS: N 38°09.77′ W 106°35.99′

▼ 0.0		Proceed along track.
8.7 ▲	SO	Cochetopa Pass marker. Then cattle guard and track on left. Zero trip meter.

▼ 1.5	SO	4WD track on left.
7.2 ▲	SO	4WD track on right.

▼ 1.7	SO	4WD track on left.
7.0 ▲	SO	4WD track on right.

▼ 2.3	SO	Cattle guard.
6.4 ▲	SO	Cattle guard.

▼ 3.2	SO	Track on right.
5.5 ▲	SO	Track on left.

▼ 4.6	SO	Cattle guard.
4.1 ▲	SO	Cattle guard.

▼ 5.2	SO	Cattle guard.
3.5 ▲	SO	Cattle guard.

▼ 6.1	SO	17 FF (FR 787) on left.
2.6 ▲	SO	17 FF (FR 787) on right.
		GPS: N 38°10.76′ W 106°41.05′

▼ 7.2	SO	17 GG (FR 804) on right.
1.5 ▲	SO	17 GG (FR 804) on left.

▼ 8.7		End at intersection with 15 GG on left (South-Central #20: Dome Lakes to Los Piños Pass Trail).
0.0 ▲		At intersection of NN 14 and 15 GG near Dome Lakes, zero trip meter and proceed southeast toward Cochetopa Pass.
		GPS: N 38°11.29′ W 106°43.54′

Taylor Canyon Trail

STARTING POINT Intersection of South-Central #18: Cochetopa Pass Road (NN 14) and FR 768

FINISHING POINT Intersection of Colorado 114 and County 31 CC

SC Trail #18: Cochetopa Pass Road

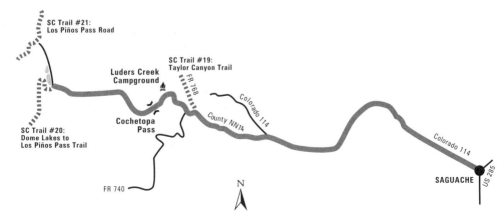

TOTAL MILEAGE 9.8 miles
UNPAVED MILEAGE 9.8 miles
DRIVING TIME 1 hour
ROUTE ELEVATION 9,980 to 8,750 feet
USUALLY OPEN Late June to early November
DIFFICULTY RATING 2
SCENIC RATING 8

Special Attractions
- Little-used, varied 4WD trail in a scenic setting.
- Good backcountry camping.
- Spring wildflowers.

Description
Taylor Canyon is a little-used side road from Cochetopa Pass Road. It offers an endless selection of good backcountry camping spots.

The route commences at the intersection of FR 770 and Cochetopa Pass Road and stretches through rolling grasslands and pine and aspen forest before traveling through the very scenic rock formations of the canyon. The area is carpeted with wildflowers in late spring and early summer.

Current Road Conditions
Rio Grande National Forest
Saguache Ranger District
46525 State Hwy 114
Saguache, CO 81149
(719) 655-2547

Map References
USFS Rio Grande NF
USGS Saguache County #1
Trails Illustrated, #139
The Roads of Colorado, p. 117
Colorado Atlas & Gazetteer, p. 69

Route Directions

▼ 0.0   From South-Central #18: Cochetopa Pass Road (NN 14) turn onto FR 768. Zero trip meter and proceed toward Taylor Canyon.
         GPS: N 38°09.55′ W 106°32.70′

▼ 0.3   SO   FR 750.2B on the right. Stay on FR 768.
▼ 1.6   SO   Through gated fence (leave it as you found it).
▼ 2.1   TR   T-intersection. Turn onto FR 770. (FR 768 goes to the left and winds around

Rock formations in Taylor Canyon

SC Trail #19: Taylor Canyon Trail

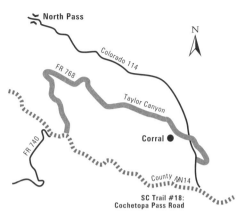

to rejoin NN 14 closer to Luders Creek Campground. Right goes through Taylor Canyon and eventually back to 114.)
GPS: N 38°11.12' W 106°33.12'

▼ 2.2   SO   Another track on the left.
▼ 3.6   UT   Another track straight ahead along canyon rim. U-turn to the right down into the canyon.
GPS: N 38°11.02' W 106°31.86'

▼ 5.4   BR   Very faint track joins in on left.
▼ 6.5   SO   Fence and gate (leave it as you found it). Rio Grande National Forest sign.
GPS: N 38°10.08' W 106°29.49'

▼ 7.3   SO   Corral in good condition on right. Then horse trough.
GPS: N 38°09.80' W 106°28.76'

▼ 8.0   SO   Colorado 114 underpass.
GPS: N 38°09.48' W 106°28.21'

▼ 8.1   SO   Colorado 114. Track on left rejoins Colorado 114.
▼ 8.9   TR   T-intersection.
GPS: N 38°08.98' W 106°27.73'

▼ 9.1   TR   Three-way intersection.
▼ 9.8   Cattle guard. Stop sign at Colorado 114.
GPS: N 38°08.87' W 106°28.01'

Dome Lakes to Los Piños Pass Trail

STARTING POINT Intersection South-Central #18: Cochetopa Pass Road (NN 14) and County 15 GG
FINISHING POINT Intersection of South-Central #21: Los Piños Pass Trail (FR 788) and FR 790, 1 mile east of the pass
TOTAL MILEAGE 29.5 miles
UNPAVED MILEAGE 29.5 miles
DRIVING TIME 1 1/2 hours
ROUTE ELEVATION 11,600 to 9,196 feet
USUALLY OPEN Early June to mid-November
DIFFICULTY RATING 2
SCENIC RATING 7

Special Attractions
- Fairly easy 4WD trail through attractive countryside.
- Relatively light traffic.
- Historic old stagecoach route.
- Good backcountry camping.
- Can be combined with South-Central #21 to form a loop.

Description
This trail provides the option of a loop tour by using Los Piños Pass Road (South-Central #21) to return from Los Piños Pass rather than proceeding through to Lake City or north toward Gunnison.

Old cowboy accommodations

It is an easy drive and could be confidently undertaken in most passenger cars, as long as the road is dry. Navigation is not difficult, and the region has the decided advantage over many other trails in this book of being uncrowded, except in hunting season.

The route runs along a historic stagecoach route from Saguache to the San Juan Mountains. It travels through varied but mainly gentle, scenic countryside with broad open meadows interspersed with forest, including many stands of aspen that add to the beauty of the area in the fall.

Numerous backcountry campsites with plenty of space and good access to water and firewood are to be found along the route.

Current Road Conditions

Gunnison National Forest
Gunnison Ranger District
216 North Colorado
Gunnison, CO 81230
(970) 641-0471

Map References

USFS   Gunnison NF

USGS   Saguache County #1
          Saguache County #3
Trails Illustrated, #139
The Roads of Colorado, pp. 116-117
Colorado Atlas & Gazetteer, p. 68

Route Directions

▼ 0.0   At intersection of South-Central #18: Cochetopa Pass Road (NN 14) and County 15 GG, zero trip meter and proceed south on 15 GG (at southern tip of Dome Lakes).

15.9 ▲   End at intersection of 15 GG and NN 14. South-Central #18: Cochetopa Pass Road commences to the right.
          GPS: N 38°11.32' W 106°43.58'

▼ 0.8   SO Track on right.
15.1 ▲   SO Track on left.

▼ 0.9   SO Access to wild trout stream on right. Cattle guard.
15.0 ▲   SO Cattle guard. Access to wild trout stream on left.

▼ 2.6   SO Cattleyards on right.

Rock formations along Dome Lakes to Los Piños Pass Trail

SC Trail #20: Dome Lakes to Los Piños Pass Trail

13.3 ▲ SO Cattleyards on left.

▼ 4.0 BR Cattle guard. Road on left is 14 DD.
11.9 ▲ BL Road on right is 14 DD. Cattle guard.

▼ 4.4 SO Cross over two creeks. Seasonal gate. Three old buildings on right.
11.5 ▲ SO Three old buildings on left; then seasonal gate and cross over two creeks.
GPS: N 38°09.20' W 106°45.66'

▼ 7.9 SO Historic Stage Route sign on right. Road on right is 790.1F.
8.0 ▲ SO Road on left is 790.1F. Historic Stage Route sign on left.
GPS: N 38°08.41' W 106°48.28'

▼ 8.3 BL Track on right.
7.6 ▲ BR Track on left.

▼ 11.0 SO Cross over Pauline Creek.
4.9 ▲ SO Cross over Pauline Creek.

▼ 13.4 SO Cross over Perfecto Creek.
2.5 ▲ SO Cross over Perfecto Creek.

▼ 13.7 SO Cattle guard. Corral on left off in distance (0.5 mile).
2.2 ▲ SO Cattle guard.

▼ 15.9 TR Road splits. Sign. Zero trip meter.
0.0 ▲ Continue along track.
GPS: N 38°03.66' W 106°51.28'

▼ 0.0 Continue along track.
13.6 ▲ TL Intersection. Zero trip meter.

▼ 0.9 BR Track forks.
12.7 ▲ BL Intersection.

▼ 1.4 SO Cross over Perfecto Creek.
12.2 ▲ SO Cross over Perfecto Creek.

▼ 1.9 BR Track on left.
11.7 ▲ BL Track on right.

▼ 2.6 SO Track on left. Entering Big Meadows.
11.0 ▲ SO Track on right. Leave Big Meadows.

▼ 3.0 SO Cross over Pauline Creek.
10.6 ▲ SO Cross over Pauline Creek.

▼ 3.9	TL	Onto Big Meadows Road (FR 790).	
9.7 ▲	TR	Onto FR 794. Entering Big Meadows.	
		GPS: N 38°05.32' W 106°53.28'	

▼ 5.2	SO	Tracks on left and right.
8.4 ▲	SO	Tracks on left and right.

▼ 6.0	SO	Cattle guard.
7.6 ▲	SO	Cattle guard.

▼ 6.2	SO	FR 7901M on right (timber harvest road closed and gated). Entering Willow Park.
7.4 ▲	SO	Leaving Willow Park. FR 7901M on left.

▼ 6.7	SO	Leaving Willow Park.
6.9 ▲	SO	Entering Willow Park.

▼ 7.7	SO	Cross over East Los Piños Creek. Cebolla Trailhead on left.
5.9 ▲	SO	Cebolla Trailhead on right. Cross over East Los Piños Creek.
		GPS: N 38°03.64' W 106°55.94'

▼ 9.0	SO	Cross over creek.
4.6 ▲	SO	Cross over creek.

▼ 10.0	SO	Cattle guard.
3.6 ▲	SO	Cattle guard.

▼ 11.4	SO	Track on left. Entering Groundhog Park.
2.2 ▲	SO	Leaving Groundhog Park. Track on right.

▼ 11.5	SO	Leaving Groundhog Park.
2.1 ▲	SO	Entering Groundhog Park.

▼ 12.0	SO	Tracks to left and right. Continue on FR 790.
1.6 ▲	SO	Continue on FR 790. Tracks to left and right.

▼ 13.1	SO	Seasonal closure gate.
0.5 ▲	SO	Seasonal closure gate.

▼ 13.6		T-Intersection with South-Central #21:

		Los Piños Pass Road (FR 788).
0.0 ▲		At intersection of South-Central #21: Los Piños Pass Road (FR 788) and Big Meadows Road (FR 790), zero trip meter and proceed along FR 790.
		GPS: N 38°06.27' W 106°57.34'

Los Piños Pass Road

STARTING POINT Cathedral Junction-intersection of FR 788 (County 15) and County 5
FINISHING POINT Doyleville at intersection of US 50 and County 45
TOTAL MILEAGE 44.6 miles
UNPAVED MILEAGE 43.3 miles
DRIVING TIME 1 3/4 hours
ROUTE ELEVATION 10,450 to 9,700 feet
USUALLY OPEN Early June to mid-November
DIFFICULTY RATING 1
SCENIC RATING 7

Special Attractions

- Easy, scenic route.
- Aspen viewing in the fall.
- Historic stagecoach route.
- Numerous backcountry campsites.
- Can be combined with South-Central #20 to form a loop.

History

Los Piños is Spanish for "the pine trees." The pass was a well-used Ute trail. Los Piños Indian Agency was established after various bands of Ute were relocated to this area from the San Luis Valley. This agency is now a forest service work center located on this route.

The Hayden survey party crossed the pass in 1874 on its way to examine the Cebolla Creek area. Otto Mears built the Saguache and San Juan toll road over the pass road the same year. Stagecoaches ran from Saguache along this road, branching north to the Gunnison River and across to Montrose and south to Lake City.

A view of Los Piños Pass Road

Description

This is a delightful, easy route through pine and aspen forest and open meadows. Backcountry campsites abound, and except in hunting season, the area is lightly used.

This easily navigated route starts at the intersection of Los Piños Pass Road (FR 788) and Hinsdale County 5 at Cathedral Junction. The pass is only six miles east from this point along an easy, 2WD road. Los Piños Pass is a gentle, wooded crossing.

One mile past the summit, FR 790 turns off to the right toward Dome Lakes (South-Central #20). This route continues along FR 788 for another twelve miles to the old Los Piños Indian Agency before intersecting with Colorado 114. You travel north on 114 for only about a mile before turning right onto the well-maintained gravel road to Doyleville, an old Denver & Rio Grande railroad station and small supply town on the route from Salida.

Current Road Conditions

Gunnison National Forest
Gunnison Ranger District
216 North Colorado
Gunnison, CO 81230
(970) 641-0471

Map References

USFS   Gunnison NF
USGS   Saguache County #1
            Saguache County #3
            Hinsdale County #1
            Gunnison County #5
Trails Illustrated, #139
The Roads of Colorado, pp. 101, 116-117
Colorado Atlas & Gazetteer, pp. 68-69

Route Directions

▼ 0.0   At intersection of FR 788 and Hinsdale County 5 in Cathedral Junction, zero trip meter and proceed toward Los Piños Pass.

5.7   End at intersection of FR 788 and

THE KIT CARSON TREATY WITH THE UTE INDIANS

In the 1860s, the Ute maintained an uneasy peace with the whites who were slowly encroaching on their lands. The initial fur trapping and prospecting had not greatly affected the Ute way of life, but numerous gold discoveries from 1858 to 1860 led to greater incursions of white settlers into Ute territory.

In 1868, in response to the influx of miners and continued pressure for land to settle, a treaty known as the Kit Carson Treaty was negotiated by Chief Ouray, whereby the Ute gave up their land in the central Rockies and San Luis Valley and agreed to be settled on 16 million acres of land in western Colorado. This reservation was a rectangle that sat against the western and southern borders of the state, with its eastern border reaching almost to where Gunnison and Steamboat Springs are presently located, and its northern border located just south of the Yampa River.

Chief Ouray in 1877

Two agencies, the White River Agency and the Los Piños Agency, were established in 1869 to maintain the reservation and to distribute the promised $50,000 worth of supplies to the Ute every year.

County 5 in Cathedral Junction.
Note: left goes to Lake City and right to Powderhorn and Gunnison.
GPS: N 38°05.74' W 107°01.99'

▼ 1.1   BL   Seasonal gate and intersection.
4.6 ▲   BR   Seasonal gate and intersection.
GPS: N 38°05.09' W 107°01.17'

▼ 5.7   SO   Summit of Los Piños Pass. Zero trip meter.
0.0 ▲   Proceed along FR 788.
GPS: N 38°06.26' W 106°58.28'

▼ 0.0   Proceed along FR 788.
18.3 ▲   SO   Summit of Los Piños Pass. Zero trip meter.

▼ 0.5   SO   Track on left.
17.8 ▲   SO   Track on right.

▼ 1.0   SO   South-Central #20 (FR 790) on right.
17.3 ▲   SO   South-Central #20 (FR 790) on left.
GPS: N 38°06.27' W 106°57.34'

▼ 2.0   SO   Beaver pond on right. Road on right.
16.3 ▲   SO   Road on left. Beaver pond on left.

▼ 2.6   SO   FR 599 on left.
15.7 ▲   SO   FR 599 on right.

▼ 5.5   SO   Creek crossing.
12.8 ▲   SO   Creek crossing.

▼ 7.2   SO   Seasonal closure gate.
11.1 ▲   SO   Seasonal closure gate.

▼ 7.3   SO   McDonough Reservoir (0.5 mile) turnoff on left.
11.0 ▲   SO   McDonough Reservoir (0.5 mile) turnoff on right.

▼ 7.5   SO   Track on left.
10.8 ▲   SO   Track on right.

▼ 8.7   SO   Track on left.
9.6 ▲   SO   Track on right.

▼ 9.5   SO   Road on right is FR 790/County Road 8 EE.
8.8 ▲   SO   Road on left is FR 790/County Road 8 EE.
GPS: N 38°10.21' W 106°51.18'

▼ 11.0   SO   Historic Stage Route sign. FR 808 on left (gated-no access).
7.3 ▲   SO   FR 808 on right. Historic Stage Route sign.

▼ 11.9   SO   Mine remains on left. Leaving National Forest sign.
6.4 ▲   SO   Entering National Forest sign. Mine remains on right.

SC Trail #21: Los Piños Pass Road

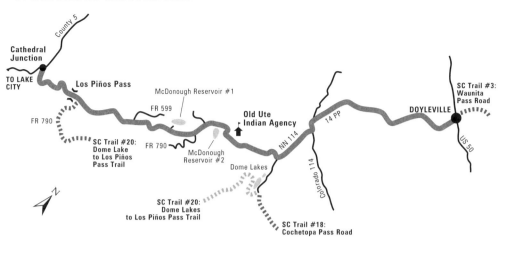

▼ 12.7   SO   Old Agency Guard Station. Cattle guard.

5.6 ▲   SO   Cattle guard. Old Agency Guard Station.
GPS: N 38°11.95′ W 106°49.69′

▼ 18.3   TL   T-Intersection with NN 14 and KK 14. Zero trip meter.

0.0 ▲   Proceed along KK 14.
GPS: N 38°13.99′ W 106°44.80′

▼ 0.0   Proceed along NN 14.

20.6 ▲   TR   Onto KK 14. Zero trip meter.

▼ 2.5   SO   Moss Lake on left.

18.1 ▲   SO   Moss Lake on right.

▼ 3.3   TL   Cattle guard. T-Intersection with Colorado 114.

17.3 ▲   TR   Intersection with NN 14.
GPS: N 38°16.63′ W 106°44.10′

▼ 4.6   TR   Onto 14 PP to Doyleville.

16.0 ▲   TL   Onto Colorado 114.

▼ 13.9   SO   Creek crossing and cattle guard.

6.7 ▲   SO   Cattle guard and creek crossing.

▼ 14.4   SO   18 VV on left.

6.2 ▲   SO   18 VV on right.

▼ 18.1   SO   18 VV on left. Cattle guard.

2.5 ▲   SO   Cattle guard. 18 VV on right.

▼ 20.6   Doyleville. End at T-Intersection with US 50.

0.0 ▲   At intersection of US 50 and County 45 in Doyleville, zero trip meter and proceed south along County 45.
GPS: N 38°27.14′ W 106°36.48′

SOUTH-CENTRAL REGION TRAIL #22

Schofield Pass and Devil's Punchbowl Trail

STARTING POINT Mount Crested Butte
FINISHING POINT Marble
TOTAL MILEAGE 21.2 miles
UNPAVED MILEAGE 20.1 miles
DRIVING TIME 3 1/2 hours
ROUTE ELEVATION 10,707 to 8,000 feet
USUALLY OPEN Late July to mid-September
DIFFICULTY RATING 6
SCENIC RATING 10

Special Attractions
- Famous and dangerous 4WD trail along an old stagecoach route.

- Historic mill on Crystal River.
- Ghost towns of Gothic and Crystal and town site of Schofield.
- Can be combined with South-Central #25: Kebler Pass Road to form a loop.

History

Schofield Pass was named for Judge B. F. Schofield, who founded the town of Schofield. Ute Indians used the pass, and they led the first white men across it. Prospectors traveled the pass frequently during the 1870s, although the first big strikes in the area did not occur until around 1880. In the mid-1870s, the Hayden survey party crossed Schofield Pass and plotted it on its map.

By the early 1880s, the cities of Marble, Crystal, Schofield, and Gothic were all at their peak. The pass road was heavily used but was never improved beyond a rough, narrow wagon road. Nonetheless, a stage ran from Crested Butte to Crystal for a number of years. This small road's political apogee came when it was traveled by President Ulysses S. Grant during his visit to many of the mining camps in the area, accompanied by John Routt, the last appointed governor of the territory and the first elected governor of the state.

The township of Gothic was established in 1879, with the discovery of gold and silver ores in the area. Within four months, nearly two hundred buildings had been erected, including a hotel, three stores, a butcher shop, a barber shop, and a saloon. Millions of dollars' worth of gold and silver ores were extracted from the hills. At its peak, the bustling mining city had a population of around eight thousand.

Gothic gained a reputation as a very wild town with lots of drinking, gambling, and prostitution. When, on his trip through the area in 1880, Ulysses S. Grant asked to see a wild mining town, he was shown Gothic. He reportedly drove his own stage into town and arrived to a riotous celebration.

Gothic's first mayor was elected by a roll of dice between two men. The winner was Garwood Judd, one of the town's saloon-keepers. After gold and silver played out, fortunes receded quickly; by 1884, most of the residents had left town. Garwood Judd remained there by himself until his death in 1930, earning himself the reputation of "the man who stayed." He was proud of his title and even nailed a plaque engraved with the phrase over his door. His ashes were scattered around the town.

Schofield was platted in August 1879 by B. F. Schofield and his party. Prospectors discovered silver in the area as early as 1872, but their fear of Indians deferred permanent settlement for several years. A smelter was built in 1880, and a mill in 1881. By 1882, the town had a population of about four hundred and the usual amenities of a hotel, a restaurant (whose staff had trouble boiling water because of the altitude), a general store, a blacksmith shop, and a barbershop.

When former President Ulysses S. Grant and former governor Routt visited Schofield, the residents of Schofield thought that if they could sell shares in one of the local mines to Grant, they could boast that the president owned a mine in Schofield. When that failed, they tried to unsuccessfully "lose" shares to Grant in a poker game—to no avail. Finally, they brought out a big barrel of whiskey, hoping to get Grant drunk and just give him the mining shares! Needless to say, Grant was impressed with Schofield's hospitality, but it is unclear whether he ended up with any claim.

Unfortunately, the ore found around Schofield was poor in quality. Although min-

A warning sign at the start of the descent through Crystal River Canyon

ers did find some good galena, the inaccessible location and high transportation costs drained off their profits. These factors, coupled with the immense problems of eight-month winters dumping as much as forty feet of snow, led to the demise of Schofield. The post office closed in 1885.

Crystal began as a silver mining camp in 1880. Early prospectors named the town after the crystal-like quartz they found along the creek. In the mid-1880s, Crystal had a population of about five hundred, a newspaper, a general store, many private homes, several saloons, and the Crystal Club (a men's club), which still stands in town.

The trail to Crystal was arduous, leading from Crested Butte over Schofield Pass. The difficulty of traversing this trail made it economically impossible to transport anything but the richest ores in or out of Crystal. Eventually, a better road was constructed, connecting the town with Carbondale.

An embedded rock that presents an obstacle along the canyon road

Although Crystal survived the silver crash of 1893, its population was reduced to a small number of residents. The much-photographed Crystal Mill remains standing on the outskirts of town along the Crystal River. The mill was built by G. C. Eaton and supplied power to the local mines. A waterwheel turned an air compressor to supply air for drilling and power for a stamp mill and sawmill.

Special Note on the Difficulty of this Road

The road through Crystal River Canyon down to the area known as the Devil's Punch Bowl is known as one of the most dangerous 4WD roads in Colorado. The road's reputation is well deserved in light of the alarming number of fatalities that have occurred on it. The most tragic was in 1970, when seven members of one family perished when their Suburban plunged from the shelf road down a two-hundred-foot drop-off and into the river. Many accidents have taken additional lives in the years since. Seven vehicles slipped off the road in the summer of 1997, and at least one of these accidents resulted in fatalities.

It is hard to dispute statistics like these, but most experienced four-wheelers will be puzzled by such a record. Certainly the road is very narrow and drops off precipitously into the river; but the surface is sound, and the road is no narrower, nor the drop more frightening, than that of many other 4WD roads in the state. Undoubtedly most accidents here must be caused by a combination of factors: the driver's inexperience, the onset of fear when committed beyond the point of turning back, and perhaps even carelessness or a failure to appreciate the very small margin for error.

Another potential hazard is caused by having to cross the river immediately before starting down the canyon. Even in late summer, the water is likely to be bumper-deep and will thoroughly soak your brakes. Therefore, follow the recommendation of the large sign erected by the forest service and check that your brakes are working properly before proceeding down the canyon. Also, do not be tempted to get out of your vehicle halfway down the canyon to take a photo and leave your vehicle reliant on the park gear position.

As is the case with all the more difficult roads in this book, you should not attempt this route until you have traveled many other less-difficult roads and are certain that you will not become flustered by the steep drop-off only a foot or so from your wheels. Less-experienced drivers are well advised not to attempt this route in a full-sized vehicle.

In spite of the risk it involves, this is a very rewarding trail. If you decide to give it a go, remember to take it very slowly and carefully.

Description

The route starts in the ski resort of Mount Crested Butte. It follows a well-maintained gravel road to Gothic, now the home of the Rocky Mountain Biological Survey, which studies the wide variety of regional flora and fauna. A few well-preserved old buildings still stand. Set in a beautiful area, the town is experiencing a revival as a summer tourist and residential area.

The summit of Schofield Pass lies beyond Emerald Lake. The low, wooded summit does not offer the views that are associated with most pass summits. The road to the pass is suitable for a passenger car. From that point on until about two miles out of Marble, stream crossings and rocky sections necessitate a high-clearance vehicle.

About a mile after the summit, the town site of Schofield lies in an open meadow beside the South Fork of the Crystal River. About a mile further, you cross through a wide section of the South Fork of the Crystal River. In the later part of summer, this is unlikely to be more than bumper deep, but the streambed contains some large rocks.

Upon exiting the river, the road curves and immediately starts the

Crystal Mill in 1893

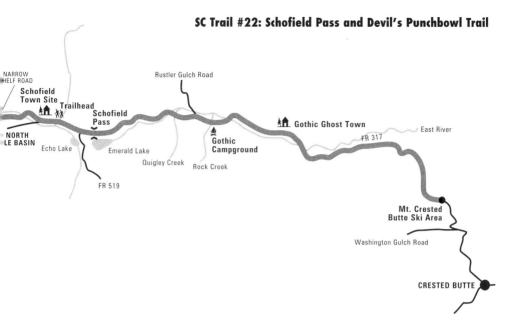

narrow, steep descent down Crystal River Canyon. Shortly after commencing the downhill run, you are confronted with a large, imbedded rock in the center of the road. You have the choice of squeezing past on the side of the rock wall or on the side of the drop-off. The road suffers from snow and rock slides, and it is not unusual to find it impassable—or at least requiring some clearance work.

At the bottom of the canyon are the Devil's Punch Bowl and, fewer than two miles farther, the township of Crystal. The powerhouse overhanging the Crystal River, called the Dead Horse Mill or the Crystal Mill, is about a quarter of a mile past Crystal on the left. The road continues past the very scenic Beaver Lake and on into Marble.

Although most years this road is open for about eight weeks, sometimes the snow does not melt and the road is closed all summer.

Current Road Conditions

White River National Forest
Sopris Ranger District
620 Main Street
Carbondale, CO 81623
(970) 963-2266

Map References

USFS Gunnison NF
USGS Gunnison County #1
      Gunnison County #2
Trails Illustrated, #128, #131, #133
The Roads of Colorado, p. 84
Colorado Atlas & Gazetteer, pp. 45-46, 58

Route Directions

▼ 0.0   In Mt. Crested Butte, where the Grand Butte Hotel walkway crosses over Gothic Road, zero trip meter and proceed north along Gothic Road.

10.6 ▲   End in Mt. Crested Butte town center.
       GPS: N 38°53.97′ W 106°57.97′

▼ 1.1   SO End of pavement. Follow main road.

9.5 ▲   SO Paved. Follow main road.
       GPS: N 38°54.77′ W 106°57.74′

▼ 1.7   SO Cattle guard. Enter National Forest (FR 317) and proceed toward Gothic.

8.9 ▲   SO Leave National Forest and proceed toward Crested Butte. Cattle guard.

▼ 3.3   SO Cattle guard.

7.3 ▲   SO Cattle guard.

▼ 4.7　SO　Bridge over East River.
5.9 ▲　SO　Bridge over East River.

▼ 5.0　SO　Bridge.
5.6 ▲　SO　Bridge.

▼ 5.1　SO　Gothic ghost town: general store and visitor center.
5.4 ▲　SO　Gothic ghost town.

▼ 5.7　SO　Track on right to Judd Falls, Trailriders, and Cooper Creek trailheads.
4.9 ▲　SO　Track on left to Judd Falls, Trailriders, and Cooper Creek trailheads.

▼ 6.5　SO　Turnoff to USFS Avery Peak picnic grounds on right.
4.1 ▲　SO　Turnoff to USFS Avery Peak picnic grounds on left.

▼ 6.7　SO　Seasonal gate and bridge.
3.9 ▲　SO　Bridge and seasonal gate.

▼ 7.0　SO　USFS Gothic Campground on left. Then track to Wash Gulch on left.
3.6 ▲　SO　Track to Wash Gulch. Then USFS Gothic Campground on right.

▼ 7.6　SO　Track to Rustler Gulch on right.
3.0 ▲　SO　Track to Rustler Gulch on left.

▼ 8.0　SO　Track on left.
2.6 ▲　SO　Track on right.

▼ 8.8　SO　Track on left.
1.8 ▲　SO　Track on right.

▼ 9.8　SO　Track on left to Emerald Lake.
0.8 ▲　SO　Track on right to Emerald Lake.

▼ 10.6　SO　Schofield Pass summit. Paradise Basin track on left; trailhead to Gothic on right. Zero trip meter.
0.0 ▲　　Continue on main road toward Gothic and Crested Butte. Leaving White River National Forest and entering Gunnison National Forest on FR 317.
GPS: N 39°00.93' W 107°02.80'

▼ 0.0　　Continue straight ahead toward

Marble. Leaving Gunnison National Forest and entering White River National Forest.
4.4 ▲　SO　Schofield Pass summit. Paradise Basin track on right; trailhead to Gothic on left. Zero trip meter.

▼ 0.7　SO　Baroni Mine portal on right. Then cross through creek.
3.7 ▲　SO　Cross through creek. Baroni Mine portal on left.

▼ 1.1　SO　Track on left to North Pole Basin.
3.3 ▲　SO　Track on right to North Pole Basin.

▼ 1.5　SO　Bridge over South Fork of Crystal River.
2.9 ▲　SO　Bridge over South Fork of Crystal River.

▼ 1.7　SO　Tracks on right.
2.7 ▲　SO　Tracks on left.

▼ 2.3　SO　Track on left to waterfall just off the road. Cross bridge with waterfall on right.
2.1 ▲　SO　Waterfall on left; cross bridge. Track on right to waterfall just off the road.

▼ 2.5　SO　Cross over river.
1.9 ▲　SO　Cross over river.

▼ 2.7　SO　Cross through wide creek.
1.7 ▲　SO　Cross through wide creek.
GPS: N 39°02.70' W 107°04.36'

▼ 2.8　SO　Tight squeeze past one large rock.
1.6 ▲　SO　Tight squeeze past one large rock.

▼ 2.8-3.2　SO　Very narrow and rocky descent.
1.2-1.6 ▲　SO　Very narrow and rocky ascent.

▼ 3.2　SO　Narrow bridge over Crystal River.
1.2 ▲　SO　Narrow bridge over Crystal River.
GPS: N 39°02.99' W 107°04.67'

▼ 4.4　BL　Intersection. Right goes to South-Central #23: Lead King Basin Trail. Zero trip meter.
0.0 ▲　　Continue on main track toward Schofield Pass, Gothic, and Crested Butte.
GPS: N 39°03.56' W 107°05.77'

▼ 0.0   Continue toward Crystal on FR 314.
4.3 ▲   BR Intersection. Left goes to South-Central
             #23: Lead King Basin Trail. Zero trip
             meter.

▼ 0.5   SO Crystal township.
3.8 ▲   SO Crystal township.

▼ 0.6   SO Cross over Crystal River.
3.7 ▲   SO Cross over Crystal River.

▼ 0.7   SO Crystal Mill on left.
3.6 ▲   SO Crystal Mill on right.
             GPS: N 39°03.56' W 107°06.22'

▼ 2.9   SO Track on left.
1.5 ▲   SO Track on right.

▼ 3.9   SO Lizard Lake on right.
0.4 ▲   SO Lizard Lake on left.
             GPS: N 39°04.19' W 107°09.21'

▼ 4.2   SO Bridge over Lost Trail Creek.
0.1 ▲   SO Bridge over Lost Trail Creek.

▼ 4.3   BL Intersection with South-Central #23:
             Lead King Basin Trail (FR 315)
             on right. Left to Marble. Zero trip
             meter.
0.0 ▲   Continue along main road.
             GPS: N 39°04.49' W 107°09.50'

▼ 0.0   Proceed toward Marble.
1.9 ▲   BR Intersection with South-Central #23:
             Lead King Basin Trail (FR 315) on left.
             Zero trip meter.

▼ 0.6   SO Road on right.
1.3 ▲   SO Road on left.

▼ 1.2   SO Beaver Lake on left.
0.7 ▲   SO Beaver Lake on right.

▼ 1.5   TL Stop sign.
0.4 ▲   TR Stop sign.

▼ 1.6   TR Intersection.
0.3 ▲   TL Intersection.

▼ 1.7   SO Bridge.
0.1 ▲   SO Bridge.

▼ 1.8   TL/TR Onto 1st Street; then right onto State
             Street.
0.1 ▲   TL/TR Onto 1st Street; then right onto Main
             Street (County 3/FR 315).

▼ 1.9   End in front of Marble Community
             Church on State Street.
0.0 ▲   On State Street in Marble, go to the
             Marble Community Church. Zero trip
             meter and proceed east.
             GPS: N 39°04.25' W 107°11.30'

SOUTH-CENTRAL REGION TRAIL #23

Lead King Basin Trail

STARTING POINT Intersection of South-Central
#22: Schofield Pass and Devil's
Punchbowl Trail (FR 314) and FR 315
FINISHING POINT Intersection of FR 315 and
FR 314
TOTAL MILEAGE 7.7 miles
UNPAVED MILEAGE 7.7 miles
DRIVING TIME 1 3/4 hours
ROUTE ELEVATION 10,800 to 8,592 feet
USUALLY OPEN Late July to mid-September
DIFFICULTY RATING 5
SCENIC RATING 8

Special Attractions

■ Abundant wildflowers in early summer.
■ The challenging, narrow, and rocky section at the east end of the route.

Description

This trail is a side road of Schofield Pass
Road. It commences 3.7 miles west of
Crystal township and 1.9 miles east of
Marble and finishes 0.5 miles east of Crystal
township.

Initially, FR 315 ascends from the road
running alongside the Crystal River (FR
314) through pine and aspen forest. The
road is bumpy with imbedded rock and
drainage channels cut across it but is not dif-

ficult in dry conditions. Sections of black soil can become very boggy after rain.

A series of switchbacks is encountered in an uphill section; but the surface is firm, and the only difficulty is caused by wheel ruts worn by other vehicles.

At about the seven-mile point the road gets considerably more difficult, especially in a full-sized vehicle, as you follow the creek cascading down into the valley. Clearances between trees and rocks are tight. The route is more difficult if attempted from east to west rather than in the direction we have described.

The area is justly famous for the wildflowers that carpet the basin in July and August, and numerous aspen provide color later in the season.

Current Road Conditions

White River National Forest
Sopris Ranger District
620 Main Street
Carbondale, CO 81623
(970) 963-2266

Map References

USFS Gunnison NF
USGS Gunnison County #1
Trails Illustrated, #128
The Roads of Colorado, p. 84
Colorado Atlas & Gazetteer, p. 46

Route Directions

▼ 0.0   At the intersection of FR 314 and FR 315 between Marble and Crystal, zero trip meter and follow sign toward Lead King Basin.

7.7 ▲   End at intersection with South-Central #22: Schofield Pass and Devil's Punchbowl Trail (FR 314) between Marble and Crystal.

GPS: N 39°04.49' W 107°09.50'

▼ 0.4   SO Private track on left to Colorado Outward Bound School.

7.3 ▲   SO Private track on right to Colorado Outward Bound School.

A section of Lead King Basin Trail

SC Trail #23: Lead King Basin Trail

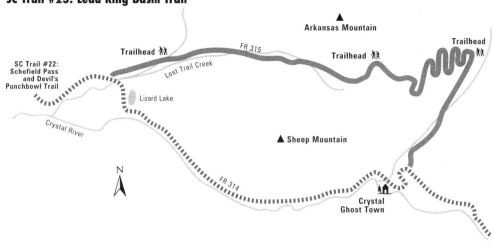

▼ 0.7   SO   North Lost Creek Trailhead on left.
Cross through North Lost Creek.

7.0 ▲   SO   Cross through North Lost Creek. North
Lost Creek Trailhead on right.

▼ 1.8   SO   Cross over creek.

5.9 ▲   SO   Cross over creek.

▼ 2.0   BL   Fork in road. Continue on FR 315.

5.7 ▲   BR   Fork in road. Continue on FR 315.

         GPS: N 39°04.68′ W 107°07.46′

▼ 2.3   SO   Cross through creek.

5.4 ▲   SO   Cross through creek.

▼ 3.7   BR   Track on left.

4.0 ▲   BL   Track on right.

▼ 4.0   SO   Cross through creek. Then track on
left.

3.7 ▲   SO   Track on right. Cross through creek.

▼ 4.1   SO   Track on left.

3.6 ▲   SO   Track on right.

▼ 6.1   SO   Cross through creek.

1.6 ▲   SO   Cross through creek.

▼ 6.2   SO   Cross through creek.

1.5 ▲   SO   Cross through creek.

▼ 6.3   SO   Trailhead parking area on left.

1.4 ▲   SO   Trailhead parking area on right.

▼ 6.5   SO   Track on left crosses through
creek.

1.2 ▲   SO   Track on right crosses through
creek.

▼ 6.6   BR   Cross bridge over creek. Bear right at
each of two intersections.

1.1 ▲   BL   Bear left at each of two intersections.
Cross bridge over creek.

▼ 6.7   SO   Cross through creek.

1.0 ▲   SO   Cross through creek.

▼ 7.7   End at intersection with FR 314.
Marble and Crystal to the right.
Schofield Pass, Crested Butte, and
Gothic to the left.

0.0 ▲   At intersection of South-Central #22:
Schofield Pass and Devil's Punchbowl
Trail (FR 314) and FR 315, zero trip
meter and proceed along FR 315.

         GPS: N 39°03.56′ W 107°05.77′

One of the many stands of aspen along this route

Ohio Pass Road

STARTING POINT Intersection of South-Central #25: Kebler Pass Road (County 12) and Ohio Pass Road (FR 730)
FINISHING POINT Gunnison
TOTAL MILEAGE 22.5 miles
UNPAVED MILEAGE 10.6 miles
DRIVING TIME 1 hour
ROUTE ELEVATION 10,300 to 7,800 feet
USUALLY OPEN Early June to mid-November
DIFFICULTY RATING 1
SCENIC RATING 6

Special Attractions

■ Gentle, easy route that follows an old railway grade.
■ Wonderful aspen viewing in fall.
■ Town site of Baldwin.

History

A wagon road opened on this old Ute Indian route in 1880. In 1882, the Denver, South Park & Pacific Railroad started laying a spur line toward Ohio Pass. However, local ore ran out before construction was completed, and the tracks were never laid beyond Ohio Pass. The railway was used to haul coal from the area for many years and was purchased by the Denver & Rio Grande Railroad in 1937. By the mid-1940s the tracks were being torn up.

The town of Baldwin came to life in 1897 with the discovery of gold nearby. In 1909, the operations shifted from gold to coal mining. Throughout the years, Baldwin was plagued by labor strikes. During one strike, union workers killed a "scab." On another occasion, strikers blew up a bridge. On Christmas Eve in 1927, a miner killed a mine superintendent over a labor dispute.

The coal mines closed in the 1940s, and

the post office discontinued service in 1949. All residents had moved from Baldwin except one man, who lived there happily until his death in 1967. Some buildings from Baldwin still exist along Ohio Pass. However, the Gunnison Chamber of Commerce advises that these buildings stand on private property, and trespassing is not allowed.

Description

Part of the route followed by FR 730 runs along the old railway grade. The route is an easy 2WD road that offers excellent views of the West Elk Mountains. The road travels through a forest thick with aspen, which turns into a sea of gold in the fall. After nearly 9 miles, the road passes the old town site of Baldwin just before becoming a paved surface. It follows the Ohio Creek into the valley before connecting to Colorado 135 about 3.5 miles from Gunnison.

Current Road Conditions

Gunnison National Forest
Gunnison Ranger District
216 North Colorado
Gunnison, CO 81230
(970) 641-0471

Map References

USFS Gunnison NF
USGS Gunnison County #2
         Gunnison County #4
Trails Illustrated, #132, #133, #134
The Roads of Colorado, p. 100
Colorado Atlas & Gazetteer, p. 58

Route Directions

▼ 0.0   At intersection of South-Central #25: Kebler Pass Road (County 12) and Ohio Pass Road (FR 730), zero trip meter and proceed south along FR 730 toward Gunnison.

10.6 ▲   End at intersection with County 12, which is South-Central #25: Kebler Pass Road.
            GPS: N 38°51.16' W 107°05.81'

▼ 4.0   SO Beaver Ponds Trailhead on right.
6.6 ▲   SO Beaver Ponds Trailhead on left.

▼ 7.9   SO FR 728 on right.
2.7 ▲   SO FR 728 on left.

▼ 8.7   SO Town site of Baldwin on left.
1.9 ▲   SO Town site of Baldwin on right.

▼ 10.6   SO FR 737 on left to Carbon Creek and to Squaw Gulch. These eventually dead-end. Zero trip meter.
0.0 ▲   Continue on main road.
            GPS: N 38°44.17' W 107°01.89'

▼ 0.0   Continue south toward Gunnison.
11.9 ▲   SO FR 737 on right to Carbon Creek and Squaw Gulch, which eventually dead-ends. Zero trip meter.

▼ 3.2   SO Road on right to Mill Creek.
8.6 ▲   SO Road on left to Mill Creek.

▼ 5.3   SO County 7 on right.

SC Trail #24: Ohio Pass Road

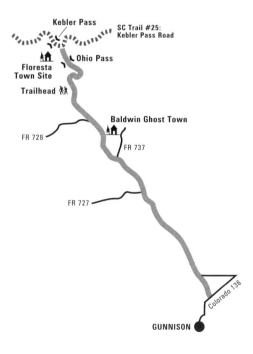

6.6 ▲	SO County 7 on left.
▼ 9.5	SO County 818 on right.
2.4 ▲	SO County 818 on left.
▼ 10.0	SO County 8 on left.
1.8 ▲	SO County 8 on right.
▼ 11.9	End at intersection with Colorado 135. Gunnison to the right; Crested Butte to the left.
0.0 ▲	At intersection of Colorado 135 and FR 730, zero trip meter and proceed north along Ohio Pass Road.
	GPS: N 38°35.50' W 106°55.05'

Kebler Pass Road

STARTING POINT Crested Butte
FINISHING POINT Intersection of Colorado 133 and County 12 near the Paonia Reservoir
TOTAL MILEAGE 29.9 miles
UNPAVED MILEAGE 27.9 miles
DRIVING TIME 1 1/4 hours
ROUTE ELEVATION 10,000 to 6,640 feet
USUALLY OPEN Late May to early October
DIFFICULTY RATING 1
SCENIC RATING 6

Special Attractions

■ Gentle, easy route that follows an old railway grade.
■ Wonderful aspen viewing in fall.
■ Irwin Cemetery.
■ Can be combined with South-Central #22: Schofield Pass and Devil's Punchbowl Trail to form a loop.

History

Kebler Pass is named for John Kebler, president of the Colorado Fuel and Iron Corporation, which owned many properties in Colorado and mined coal in the area. The pass was originally a Ute trail. The Denver & Rio Grande Railroad ran a spur line from Crested Butte to the mining town of Irwin, which was booming in the early 1880s.

Near the pass lie the townships of Ruby and Irwin, which are usually spoken of as a single community, since as each expanded, they grew together and formally united. Ruby was established in 1879, after silver was discovered at the Ruby Chief Mine. When word spread about the riches found in Ruby, prospectors poured into the camp and built cabins, even with the heavy snow on the ground. They cut down trees for their lumber; and when the snow melted in the spring, ten-foot "stumps" were everywhere!

As the town grew, it was renamed Irwin. It became one of the most important camps in Gunnison County and the principal town in the Ruby mining district. It soon became a supply center for the mining camps surrounding it in the nearby gulches and basins. Irwin had at least five hundred buildings, including seventy-five businesses. There was a large stamp mill, a sampling works, six sawmills, a bank, three churches, a theater, many hotels, and twenty-three saloons. The main street was a mile long. Irwin was so bustling that by 1880, lots that had sold the previous year for twenty-five dollars were selling for as much as five thousand dollars.

Irwin in 1882

View of Marcellina Mountain

When rumors spread that there was a plot to assassinate former President Ulysses Grant while he was giving a speech in Irwin, the speech was canceled and Grant was entertained for two days at the Irwin Club, a prestigious, members-only establishment for men. Other guests of the club included Teddy Roosevelt and Wild Bill Hickok.

As it did for other mining camps, the silver crash of 1893 led to Irwin's demise, although many mines had played out earlier. Miners and investors moved away, and by 1909 Irwin was a ghost town.

Description

Kebler Pass provides access to Crested Butte from either Grand Junction or Glenwood Springs, via Colorado 133. It also can form a loop tour from Crested Butte across Schofield Pass to Marble, then south to Paonia Reservoir, finally returning to Crested Butte over Kebler Pass. The road follows the old railway grade and is a wide, well-maintained road suitable for passenger cars.

The road offers excellent views of the Ruby Range to the north and the surrounding West Elk Mountains. In the fall, enormous stands of bright yellow aspen bring the scenery to life. The pass runs through a wooded area and does not offer the expansive views to be seen along the road.

Just east of the pass is the old Irwin Cemetery, which has about fifty graves and a commemorative marker explaining the rise and fall of the town.

Current Road Conditions

White River National Forest
Sopris Ranger District
620 Main Street
Carbondale, CO 81623
(970) 963-2266

Map References

USFS Gunnison NF
USGS Gunnison County #2
Trails Illustrated, #131, #133
The Roads of Colorado, p. 84
Colorado Atlas & Gazetteer, pp. 57-58

Route Directions

▼ 0.0   At bridge over Coal Creek on Whiterock Avenue (County 12) in Crested Butte, zero trip meter and proceed west out of town.
6.7 ▲   End in Crested Butte.
     GPS: N 38°52.11' W 106°59.35'

▼ 1.0   SO Unpaved.
5.7 ▲   SO Paved.

▼ 4.8   SO Splains Gulch turnoff on left.
1.9 ▲   SO Splains Gulch turnoff on right.

▼ 6.1   SO FR 826 on right toward Lake Irwin Campground.
0.6 ▲   SO FR 826 on left toward Lake Irwin Campground.
     GPS: N 38°51.48' W 107°05.68'

▼ 6.5   SO South-Central #24: Ohio Pass Road (FR 730) on left toward Gunnison.
0.2 ▲   SO South-Central #24: Ohio Pass Road (FR 730) turnoff on right toward Gunnison.

▼ 6.7   SO Summit of Kebler Pass. Old Irwin Cemetery on right. Zero trip meter.
0.0 ▲   Continue toward Crested Butte.
     GPS: N 38°50.97' W 107°05.99'

▼ 0.0   Continue along main road.
23.2 ▲   SO Old Irwin Cemetery on left. Summit of Kebler Pass. Zero trip meter.

▼ 1.5   SO Bridge over Ruby Anthracite Creek.
21.7 ▲   SO Bridge over Ruby Anthracite Creek.

▼ 4.3   SO Dark Canyon Trail on right and Horse Ranch Park.
18.9 ▲   SO Dark Canyon Trail on left and Horse Ranch Park.

▼ 4.5   SO Cross Ruby Anthracite Creek; then cattle guard. Cliff Creek Trail on left.
18.7 ▲   SO Cliff Creek Trail on right. Then cattle guard and cross Ruby Anthracite Creek.

▼ 8.6   SO USFS Lost Lake Campground (FR 706) on left.

14.6 ▲   SO USFS Lost Lake Campground (FR 706) on right.

▼ 10.2   SO Ruby Anthracite Trail on right.
13.0 ▲   SO Ruby Anthracite Trail on left.

▼ 14.4   SO Cattle guard.
8.8 ▲   SO Cattle guard. Enter Gunnison National Forest.

▼ 17.2   SO Paved.
6.0 ▲   SO Unpaved.

▼ 17.5   SO USFS Ericson Springs picnic area on left.
5.7 ▲   SO USFS Ericson Springs picnic area on right.

▼ 23.2   End at T-intersection with Colorado 133 near the Paonia Reservoir.
0.0 ▲   At intersection of Colorado 133 and Kebler Pass Road (County 12) near the Paonia Reservoir, zero trip meter and proceed east toward Kebler Pass.
     GPS: N 38°56.47' W 107°21.70'

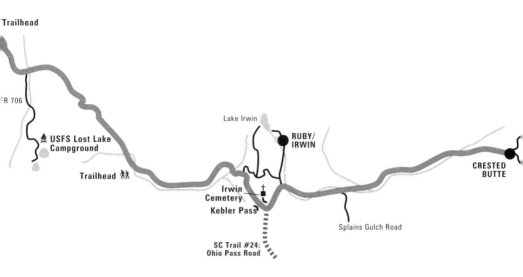

Trailhead

FR 706

USFS Lost Lake Campground

Lake Irwin

RUBY/ IRWIN

CRESTED BUTTE

Trailhead

Irwin Cemetery

Kebler Pass

Splains Gulch Road

SC Trail #24: Ohio Pass Road

SOUTH-CENTRAL REGION TRAIL #26

Reno Divide Trail

STARTING POINT Intersection of Colorado 135 and Cement Creek Road (FR 740)

FINISHING POINT Intersection of South-Central #27:Taylor Pass Trail (County/FR 742) and Italian Creek Road (FR 759)

TOTAL MILEAGE 26.3 miles

UNPAVED MILEAGE 25.8 miles

DRIVING TIME 4 hours

ROUTE ELEVATION 12,015 to 8,595 feet

USUALLY OPEN Mid-June to mid-October

DIFFICULTY RATING 4

SCENIC RATING 8

Special Attractions

■ Very scenic, varied, and moderately difficult 4WD trail.

■ Access from Crested Butte to Taylor Pass.

■ Good backcountry camping sites.

History

In 1879, prospectors crossed Pearl Pass into the Roaring Fork Valley and discovered ore near Ashcroft. In the following year, more rich ore was discovered near Aspen. By this time, the area was teeming with miners.

In 1880, a company was formed to build a road over Independence Pass from Leadville to Aspen in order to provide access to Leadville's railhead and smelters. At the same time, the pack trail over Taylor Pass, which had been used by prospectors since the previous year, was upgraded to a wagon road to provide access from Taylor Park and Buena Vista. The opening of Taylor Pass Road spurred the desire of those in Crested Butte to gain access to the new mining area. The road over Reno Divide was built to forge a stage route connection to Taylor Pass Road.

The Denver & Rio Grande Railroad spur reached Crested Butte from Gunnison in 1881. By that time, Aspen was the center of a silver boom, following the first rich ore discoveries in the Roaring Fork Valley in 1879 and the further major discoveries the follow-

Road sign along Reno Divde Trail

ing year. Crested Butte was only twenty-four miles from Aspen and sixteen miles from Ashcroft, and the railroad was determined to expand access to its new railhead from the Roaring Fork Valley. This prompted the development of Pearl Pass Road in 1882. Although more direct, this route was extremely difficult, requiring wagons to be snubbed over the pass (that is, taken apart and hauled over in pieces). Pearl Pass Road operated for only three years.

The toll road over Independence Pass from Leadville opened in 1881 and proved to be far more successful than either of the southern routes. With the arrival in Aspen of the Denver & Rio Grande Railroad in 1887 and the Colorado Midland Railroad in 1888, the two southern roads became obsolete.

Description

This route provides access from Crested Butte to Taylor Pass Road, which leads across the Continental Divide into Aspen. It provides an alternative 4WD route to the more difficult Pearl Pass.

The route starts at the intersection of Colorado 135 and Cement Creek Road (FR 740), about seven miles south of Crested Butte. For the first nine miles of the route, Cement Creek Road travels alongside the creek in a very picturesque setting. The valley alternates between very wide sections and very narrow sections: the walls close in to form a canyon just wide enough for the creek and the road to squeeze through and then open up to panoramic views. The road through this sec-

tion is easily traveled by a 2WD vehicle.

Immediately after the turn onto FR 759, the road starts to climb. Although there are some sections of shelf road, they are lined with trees and are not intimidating. The surface of the road is sound and is maintained by the Gunnison 4-Wheelers Club.

After passing through the gate at the 3.6-mile point on FR 759, the road begins to deteriorate. For about the next four miles, the road is rough and can be very muddy after rain. Even under normal conditions, the road has muddy sections scarred with potholes, but it should not present too great an obstacle for a 4WD vehicle. This is the most difficult part of the journey.

Shortly after passing above timberline, you will encounter a steep-sided but narrow, small creek crossing along an off-camber section of the track. Having negotiated this crossing in a Suburban, we can attest to it being passable in a full-sized 4WD vehicle.

The road flattens out and travels along an open alpine ridge past the Stewart and Star mines. The views of the Italian Creek Valley and the Taylor River Valley are spectacular.

As the road descends, it is a bit rough, rocky, and muddy in sections; but the surface is generally sound and should not pose any problems under normal conditions.

From the gate just after the Lilly Pond Trailhead, the road (in dry conditions) is easily navigable in a car. However, after rain it can be very muddy. There are numerous backcountry camping spots along this section.

Current Road Conditions

Gunnison National Forest
Gunnison Ranger District
216 North Colorado
Gunnison, CO 81230
(970) 641-0471

Map References

USFS Gunnison NF
USGS Gunnison County #3
Trails Illustrated, #131
The Roads of Colorado, pp. 85, 101
Colorado Atlas & Gazetteer, pp. 58-59

Route Directions

▼ 0.0   At intersection of Colorado 135 and Cement Creek Road (FR 740), zero trip meter and proceed east.

8.8 ▲   End at intersection with Colorado 135.

GPS: N 38°48.27′ W 106°53.39′

▼ 0.2 SO Cross bridge.
8.6 ▲ SO Cross bridge.

▼ 0.5 SO Unpaved.
8.3 ▲ SO Paved.

▼ 1.7 SO Farris Creek Trailhead on left.
7.1 ▲ SO Farris Creek Trailhead on right.

▼ 3.2 SO Track to USFS Summer Home Group on right.
5.6 ▲ SO Track to USFS Summer Home Group on left.

▼ 3.5 SO USFS Cement Creek Campground.
5.3 ▲ SO USFS Cement Creek Campground.

▼ 4.5 SO Seasonal closure gate.
4.3 ▲ SO Seasonal closure gate.

▼ 7.7 SO Bridge.
1.1 ▲ SO Bridge.

▼ 7.9 SO Cross over Cement Creek.
0.9 ▲ SO Cross over Cement Creek.

▼ 8.6 SO Cross through small creek.
0.2 ▲ SO Cross through small creek.

▼ 8.8 BR Intersection on right with FR 759 (Italian Creek Road) toward Reno Divide. Cement Creek Road continues straight ahead. Zero trip meter.
0.0 ▲   Proceed south along Cement Creek Road.

GPS: N 38°53.07′ W 106°47.42′

Creek crossing near Stewart Mine

SC Trail #26: Reno Divide Trail

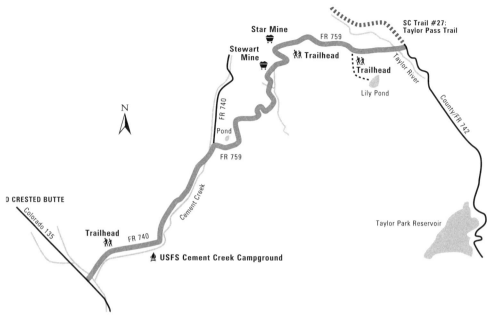

▼ 0.0   Proceed along FR 759.

9.2 ▲   TL   Intersection. Italian Creek Road and
               Cement Creek Road.

▼ 1.3   SO   Cabin ruins on left.

7.9 ▲   SO   Cabin ruins on right.

▼ 3.6   SO   Track on right. Gate. Track on left.
               Proceed through gate (leaving it as you
               found it). Follow FR 759.

5.6 ▲   SO   Track on right. Proceed through gate
               (leaving it as you found it). Follow FR
               759. Track on left.
               GPS: N 38°54.46' W 106°45.76'

▼ 5.4   SO   Cross through small, muddy creek.

3.8 ▲   SO   Cross through small, muddy creek.

▼ 5.7   SO   Cross through small creek.

3.5 ▲   SO   Cross through small creek.

▼ 6.5   SO   Pond on left and track on right (closed
               to motorized vehicles).

2.7 ▲   SO   Track on left (closed to motorized vehi-
               cles). Pond on right.

▼ 6.9   SO   Cross through creek.

2.3 ▲   SO   Cross through creek.

▼ 7.5   BR   Track on left.

1.6 ▲   BL   Track on the right is a difficult alterna-
               tive track that rejoins the road at the
               gate at mileage point 5.6 ahead.
               GPS: N 38°55.97 W 106°44.36'

▼ 7.7   SO   Cross through creek with steep sides.

1.5 ▲   SO   Cross through creek with steep sides.

▼ 7.8   SO   Cross through small creek.

1.3 ▲   SO   Cross through small creek.

▼ 8.1   SO   Stewart Mine and track to it on left.

1.1 ▲   SO   Stewart Mine and track to it on right.

▼ 8.4   SO   Stewart Mine cabin ruins on right.

0.8 ▲   SO   Stewart Mine cabin ruins on left.

▼ 8.8   BL   Track on right.

0.4 ▲   BR   Track on left.
               GPS: N 38°56.54' W 106°43.59'

▼ 8.9   BL   Fork in road. Right fork leads to
               overlook and returns to main

road in short distance.

0.3 ▲ BR Fork in road. Left fork leads to overlook and returns to main road in short distance.

▼ 9.2 BL Fork in road. Star Trailhead on the right. Zero trip meter at sign.

0.0 ▲ Continue along main track.
GPS: N 38°56.87' W 106°43.41'

▼ 0.0 Proceed toward Taylor Road.

8.3 ▲ BR Fork in road. Star Trailhead on the left. Zero trip meter at sign.

▼ 0.8 SO Track on right.

7.4 ▲ SO Track on left.

▼ 1.0 SO/BL Cabin ruins on left. Cross through small creek; then bear left past a track on the right.

7.3 ▲ BR/SO Track on the left. Cross through a small creek; then cabin ruins on right.

▼ 1.1 SO Cross through two small creeks.

7.2 ▲ SO Cross through two small creeks.

▼ 1.2 BL Mine ruins on right on private property. Follow sign toward Taylor Park.

7.1 ▲ BR Mine ruins on left. Follow sign to Cement Creek.

▼ 1.4 TR Intersection. Private road on the left.

6.9 ▲ TL Private road is straight ahead.

▼ 2.0 SO Track on right. Follow sign to Taylor Park.

6.2 ▲ SO Follow sign to Cement Creek.

▼ 2.7 SO Cross through creek.

5.5 ▲ SO Cross through creek.

▼ 4.6 SO Cross through creek.

3.7 ▲ SO Cross through creek.

▼ 5.3 SO Dorchester walking trail on left.

3.0 ▲ SO Dorchester walking trail on right.

▼ 5.5 SO Lilly Pond walking trail on right.

2.8 ▲ SO Lilly Pond walking trail on left.
GPS: N 38°57.20' W 106°40.17'

▼ 5.6 SO Gate.

2.6 ▲ SO Gate.

▼ 7.8 SO Cross bridge over Taylor River.

0.4 ▲ SO Cross bridge over Taylor River.

▼ 8.3 End at intersection with Taylor River Road (County/FR 742). Taylor Reservoir is to the right and South-Central #27:Taylor Pass Trail is to the left.

0.0 ▲ At intersection of Taylor River Road (County/FR 742) and Italian Creek Road (FR 759), zero trip meter and proceed west. along Italian Creek Road.
GPS: N 38°57.24' W 106°37.26'

SOUTH-CENTRAL REGION TRAIL #27

Taylor Pass Trail

STARTING POINT Intersection of South-Central #26: Reno Divide Trail (FR 759) and Taylor River Road (County/FR 742)
FINISHING POINT Aspen
TOTAL MILEAGE 25.3 miles
UNPAVED MILEAGE 15 miles
DRIVING TIME 2 1/2 hours
ROUTE ELEVATION 11,928 to 7,800 feet
USUALLY OPEN Early July to late September
DIFFICULTY RATING 6
SCENIC RATING 9

Special Attractions
- Very challenging 4WD trail.
- Taylor Lake, an attractive alpine lake near the summit.
- A challenging creek crossing.
- Spectacular summit views.
- Aspen viewing in the fall.

History
Taylor Pass was officially named in 1940 for mining pioneer Jim Taylor, who prospected the area as early as 1860. The pass road was instrumental in making Ashcroft, where the first ore discoveries in the Roaring Fork Valley had been made in 1879, an important

early supply center for mining in the area. The road is one of three formed in the wake of the major ore discoveries in the inaccessible Roaring Fork Valley in 1879 and 1880, as interests in Buena Vista, Crested Butte, and Leadville vied for access to the new area.

In 1880, Taylor Pass Road was built by Stevens and Company, owned by H. B. Gillespie, to haul freight into the area from Taylor Park and Buena Vista. Subsequently, the same company ran stagecoaches along the route. In 1881, a telegraph line was run over the pass.

Although the Taylor Pass route to Crested Butte was easier than the Pearl Pass route, which opened in 1882, neither were satisfactory, as freight wagons had to be "snubbed" (that is, taken apart and hauled over in pieces) to cross the pass.

When rich ore was discovered in Aspen in 1880, it became apparent that Aspen was likely to eclipse Ashcroft as the center of the mining activity in the valley. Local business interests were quick to organize the Twin Lakes and Roaring Fork Toll Company to construct a road over what is now known as Independence Pass to the smelters and railhead at Leadville. This road opened in 1881 and proved by far the most successful of the three. The need for all of the roads passed in 1887, when the Denver & Rio Grande Railroad reached Aspen, followed by the Colorado Midland Railroad the following year.

The township of Dorchester was established well after the initial flurry of activity that resulted from the discoveries in the Roaring Fork Valley. In 1900, gold was discovered in the Italian Mountains, and Dorchester became the main mining camp in the area. Despite initial optimism that swelled the population to more than one thousand, the mines were never very successful. The harsh winters made operating the mines difficult and costly. Nonetheless, some of the mines were operated year-round despite the ever-present danger of snowslides. On one occasion, fifteen were reported in a single day. Activity lingered on until World War I, helped by production of lead and zinc, but shortly afterward the mines were closed and the remaining residents moved away.

Ashcroft was settled shortly after silver strikes in 1879. Initially, the town was known as Castle Forks but was soon renamed Ashcroft. In its early days the town served as the gateway to Aspen for travelers coming over Taylor Pass or Cottonwood Pass. Established at about the same period as Aspen, Ashcroft seemed

The rocky section of Taylor Pass Trail

Taylor Lake

likely to become the more successful of the two. The Ashcroft post office was established in 1880. The town had five hotels, a newspaper, a school, a jail, a doctor, a bowling alley, several stores, and many saloons.

Two factors led to the decline of Ashcroft. One was the completion of Independence Pass, which opened accessibility to nearby Aspen. Then, in 1887, the Denver & Rio Grande completed a railway line into Aspen, which encouraged Ashcroft's residents to migrate to Aspen.

Description

The start of this 4WD route can be reached either from Crested Butte by way of the Reno Divide (South-Central #26) or from Tincup or Buena Vista by connecting with Taylor River Road (County 742) at Taylor Park Reservoir.

The route commences heading west on County 742, a well-maintained passenger

vehicle road. The turnoff to Taylor Pass (FR 761) is a little more than two miles after the town site of Dorchester. From this point, the road is 4WD, although initially it is just a bumpy road through the forest.

At the 1.6-mile point in from County 742, the trail formerly ran in the creek for about a hundred yards, requiring negotiation of the rocky streambed in water up to bumper-level. However, in the summer of 1997, the forest service rerouted the creek and leveled the road somewhat. This section had been the most difficult part of the road, particularly when water obscured large boulders. It is unclear how rough and challenging the road will be after the renovations have had time to settle.

A couple of miles farther on, after reaching timberline, the road splits into a number of alternative routes past Taylor Lake and up the final ascent to the summit. The one detailed in the directions below is the easiest and most scenic. It proceeds around the southern and western sides of Taylor Lake.

From the summit of the pass, you enter the White River National Forest. Two roads lead down to Aspen: Express Creek Road and Richmond Hill Road (FR 123). The directions follow the quicker and easier Express Creek Road via the ghost town of Ashcroft.

The initial descent is a very steep, narrow shelf road, and the gravel road surface can be loose and slippery. We recommend that you engage first or second gear in low range to avoid locking the brakes and proceed slowly. The steep descent, in two stages, lasts for about half a mile. The views from the summit and during the descent along Express Creek are magnificent. At timberline, the road enters a dense aspen forest as it continues to descend to Castle Creek Road, about one-quarter of a mile north of the ghost town of Ashcroft.

In 1974, the Aspen Historical Society leased Ashcroft's town site from the U.S. Forest Service in order to preserve the historic remains. Although some of the buildings you see there today are original, others were brought in to replace deteriorated ones so that tourists can safely explore the resurrected ghost town.

From this point, the road is paved all the way into Aspen.

Current Road Conditions
Gunnison National Forest
Gunnison Ranger District
216 North Colorado
Gunnison, CO 81230
(970) 641-0471

Map References
USFS Gunnison NF or White River NF
USGS Gunnison County #3
      Pitkin County #2
Trails Illustrated, #127, #131
The Roads of Colorado, p. 85
Colorado Atlas & Gazetteer, pp. 46, 59

Route Directions

▼ 0.0   At intersection of South-Central #26: Reno Divide Trail (FR 759) and Taylor River Road (County/FR 742), zero trip

meter and proceed northwest. This intersection is 11 miles north of Taylor Park Reservoir. Note: sign here reads "Dead end."

5.6 ▲   End at intersection with South-Central #26: Reno Divide Trail (FR 759).
         GPS: N 38°57.24' W 106°37.26'

▼ 1.8   SO Tellurium Creek Road on right.
3.8 ▲   SO Tellurium Creek Road on left.

▼ 2.4   SO Track on left to Old Dorchester Guard Station.
3.2 ▲   SO Track on right to Old Dorchester Guard Station.

▼ 2.6   SO USFS Dorchester Campground turnoff on left.
3.0 ▲   SO USFS Dorchester Campground turnoff on right.

▼ 2.9   SO Fishing Access Road on left.
2.7 ▲   SO Fishing Access Road on right.

▼ 5.5   SO Cattle guard.
0.1 ▲   SO Cattle guard.

▼ 5.6   TR Onto Taylor Pass Road (FR 761). Zero trip meter.
0.0 ▲   Proceed on FR 742.
         GPS: N 38°59.73' W 106°42.17'

▼ 0.0   Proceed onto FR 761.

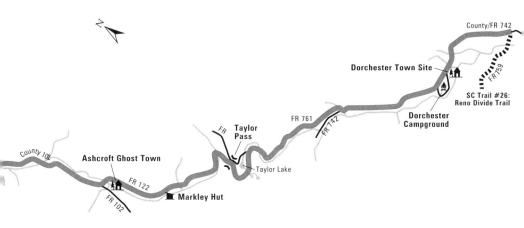

3.4 ▲   TL   Intersection: FR 761 and Taylor River Road (FR 742). Zero trip meter.

▼ 1.4   SO   Cross through creek.
2.0 ▲   SO   Cross through creek.

▼ 1.5   BR   Fork in road.
1.9 ▲   BL   Fork in road.

▼ 1.6   SO   Road follows the path of the old creek bed. Note: In the summer of 1997, the creek was diverted from this section to the east side of the road.
1.8   SO   Road follows the path of the old creek bed.

▼ 2.9   SO   Cross through creek.
0.5 ▲   SO   Cross through creek.

▼ 3.4   TL   Fork in road with sign to Taylor Pass Divide Road. 761.1A on left; 761.1 to the right. Zero trip meter.
0.0 ▲   Proceed on FR 761.
      GPS: N 39°01.04′ W 106°44.92′

▼ 0.0   Proceed along 761.1A.
1.4 ▲   TR   Fork in road. Zero trip meter.

▼ 0.1   SO   Taylor Lake on right.
1.3 ▲   SO   Taylor Lake on left.

▼ 0.5   SO   Ponds on left.
0.9 ▲   SO   Ponds on right.

▼ 0.6   BR   Fork in road. Follow sign to Taylor Pass.
0.8 ▲   SO   Follow sign to "Taylor Pass Road #761, 1 mile."
      GPS: N 39°00.71′ W 106°45.42′

▼ 0.7   SO   Cross through creek.
0.7 ▲   SO   Cross through creek.

▼ 1.4   BL   Taylor Pass. Zero trip meter.
0.0 ▲   BR   Proceed from summit on the track to the southwest, which descends from the left-hand side of the "Taylor Pass" sign, entering Gunnison National Forest.
      GPS: N 39°01.21′ W 106°45.32′

▼ 0.0   BL   Proceed on the track (FR 122) that descends from the right hand side of the "Taylor Pass" sign, entering White River National Forest. Follow Express Creek Road (FR 122) toward Ashcroft.
4.6 ▲   BR   Taylor Pass. Zero trip meter.

▼ 0.6   SO   Bridge over Express Creek.
4.0 ▲   SO   Bridge over Express Creek.

▼ 2.2   SO   Cross through creek.
2.4 ▲   SO   Cross through creek.

▼ 2.7   SO   Track on left to Markley Hut.
1.8 ▲   SO   Track on right to Markley Hut.
      GPS: N 39°02.21′ W 106°47.26′

▼ 4.0	SO	Cross through creek.
0.6 ▲	SO	Cross through creek.
▼ 4.2	SO	Private track on left.
0.4 ▲	SO	Private track on right.
▼ 4.4	SO	Bridge over Castle Creek.
0.2 ▲	SO	Bridge over Castle Creek.
▼ 4.6	TR	Intersection with Castle Creek Road (FR 102). The restored ghost town of Ashcroft is just to the left. Zero trip meter.
0.0 ▲		Proceed toward Taylor Pass on Express Creek Road.

GPS: N 39°03.63′ W 106°48.03′

▼ 0.0		Proceed north along Castle Creek Road toward Aspen.
10.3 ▲	TL	Intersection: Castle Creek Road (FR 102) and Express Creek Road (County 15 C). The restored ghost town of Ashcroft is 0.4 miles south. Zero trip meter.
▼ 10.3	TR	Intersection with County 13. Then almost immediately is the intersection with Colorado 82. Aspen is to the right. End of trail.
0.0 ▲		At the intersection of Colorado 82 and County 13 in Aspen, zero trip meter and proceed southwest. Almost immediately turn left onto Castle Creek Road.

GPS: N 39°11.74′ W 106°50.39′

SOUTH-CENTRAL REGION TRAIL #28

Hayden Pass Trail

STARTING POINT: Villa Grove
FINISHING POINT: Intersection of Hayden Creek Road (County 6) and US 50
TOTAL MILEAGE: 15.8 miles
UNPAVED MILEAGE: 14.4 miles
DRIVING TIME: 1 1/2 hours
ROUTE ELEVATION: 10,870 to 6,590 feet

USUALLY OPEN: Early July to mid-October
DIFFICULTY RATING: 3
SCENIC RATING: 7

Special Attractions
■ One of the few 4WD trails in the Sangre de Cristo Range.
■ Varied 4WD route with good views, particularly of the San Luis Valley.
■ Can be combined with South-Central #29 across Medano Pass to form a loop.

History
This pass was another used by the Ute to cross between the San Luis Valley and the Arkansas River to the northeast. In 1874, a wagon road was built across the pass, and Ferdinand Hayden noted this road when his survey party crossed it in 1875. The pass is officially named for an early settler of the Wet Mountain Valley, Lewis Hayden.

By the late 1870s, Hayden Pass was a popular route to Villa Grove—an important supply center at that time to the main route west via Cochetopa Pass and to the mining area of Bonanza, some seventeen miles northwest. It connected to the network of toll roads built by Otto Mears over the Cochetopa, Los Piños, and Poncha Passes. Mears built one of his first toll roads between Villa Grove and Bonanza, alongside Kerber Creek.

Villa Grove, established in 1870 as Garibaldi, was nestled in a grove of trees. In 1872, the name was changed to Villagrove, which was subsequently broken into two words. A narrow-gauge spur line of the Denver & Rio Grande Railroad terminated at Villa Grove prior to being extended to Alamosa in 1890.

Description
The route heads east from Villa Grove, but the turnoff is unmarked except for a "Villa Grove Common" sign. The road initially travels through the ranch land of the San Luis Valley before starting its ascent toward the pass.

The route is easy to navigate but has a few

The road on the east side of Hayden Pass

sections, mainly on the east side, that are steep and quite rough and require high clearance. It travels through pine forest most of the way but provides some good views along the route, particularly the sweeping views back across the San Luis Valley.

The route passes Rainbow Trail, a 55-mile hiking trail, and two U.S. Forest Service campgrounds before reaching US 50 at Coaldale, 4.1 miles west of Cotopaxi and 20 miles south of Salida.

Current Road Conditions
San Isabel National Forest
Salida Ranger District
325 West Rainbow Boulevard
Salida, CO 81201
(719) 539-3591

Map References
USFS Rio Grande NF
      San Isabel NF

USGS Saguache #2
      Fremont #1
The Roads of Colorado, p. 119
Colorado Atlas & Gazetteer, pp. 70-71

Route Directions

▼ 0.0		At intersection of US 285 and County LL 57 (FR 970) in Villa Grove, zero trip meter and proceed east along LL 57.
6.9 ▲		End at intersection with US 285 in Villa Grove.
		GPS: N 38°14.96′ W 105°56.92′

▼ 0.1	SO	Cattle guard and sign to Hayden Pass.
6.8 ▲	SO	Cattle guard.

▼ 1.6	SO	Cross over San Luis Creek.
5.3 ▲	SO	Cross over San Luis Creek.

▼ 2.7	SO	Cattle guard. County 60 MM on left.
4.2 ▲	SO	County 60 MM on right. Cattle guard.

SC Trail #28: Hayden Pass Trail

▼ 2.8　SO　Track on right.
4.1 ▲　SO　Track on left.

▼ 4.1　SO　Track on left.
2.8 ▲　SO　Track on right.

▼ 4.2　SO　Track on right.
2.7 ▲　SO　Track on left.

▼ 4.6　SO　Enter Rio Grande National Forest.
2.3 ▲　SO　Leave Rio Grande National Forest.
　　　　GPS: N 38°16.84' W 105°52.30'

▼ 6.9　SO　Summit of Hayden Pass. Zero trip meter.
0.0 ▲　　　Continue. Enter Rio Grande National Forest. Name of road changes to FR 970.
　　　　GPS: N 38°17.60' W 105°50.95'

▼ 0.0　　　Continue. Enter San Isabel National Forest. Name of road changes to FR 64.
8.9 ▲　SO　Summit of Hayden Pass. Zero trip meter.

▼ 1.1　SO　Track on left.
7.8 ▲　SO　Track on right.

▼ 1.5　SO　Cabin on right.
7.4 ▲　SO　Cabin on left.

▼ 1.9　SO　Track on left.
7.0 ▲　SO　Track on right.

▼ 2.0　SO　Track on left.
6.9 ▲　SO　Track on right.

▼ 2.8　SO　Track on left.
6.1 ▲　SO　Track on right.

▼ 4.1　TR　Intersection. San Isabel National Forest Campground entrance and Rainbow Trail walking track straight ahead. Turn onto County 6 (FR 006) toward Coaldale.
4.8 ▲　TL　Intersection. San Isabel National Forest Campground entrance and Rainbow Trail walking track. Turn onto FR 64.
　　　　GPS: N 38°19.79' W 105°49.36'

▼ 5.4　SO　USFS Coaldale Campground on right.
3.5 ▲　SO　USFS Coaldale Campground on left.

▼ 8.6　SO　Paved road on left.
0.3 ▲　SO　Paved road on right.

▼ 8.9　　　End at intersection with US 50.
0.0 ▲　　　Intersection: US 50 and County 6, at Coaldale. Sign: "NF Access Hayden Creek." Zero trip meter and proceed south along County 6 (FR 006), also called Hayden Creek Road.
　　　　GPS: N 38°22.06' W 105°45.11'

SOUTH-CENTRAL REGION TRAIL #29

Medano Pass and Great Sand Dunes Trail

STARTING POINT Intersection of Colorado 69 and FR 559

FINISHING POINT Tollbooth for Great Sand Dunes National Monument on Colorado 150

TOTAL MILEAGE 21.6 miles

UNPAVED MILEAGE 20.1 miles

Medano Creek crossing

DRIVING TIME 2 hours
ROUTE ELEVATION: 9,940 to 7,706 feet
USUALLY OPEN Late May to late October
DIFFICULTY RATING 4
SCENIC RATING 10

Special Attractions
- The spectacular Great Sand Dunes National Monument with much more scenic access than the paved roads.
- Four-wheel driving through sand and numerous creek crossings.
- Historic pass route that can be combined with South-Central #28 across Hayden Pass to form a loop.

History
Medano means "sand hill" in Spanish, and the pass was also known as Sandhill Pass.

In 1807, Zebulon Pike crossed the pass after his famous attempt to climb the fourteen-thousand-foot peak that bears his name. By the 1850s, the pass was much used by fur traders and the mountain men heading for the San Juan region of Colorado. Captain John Gunnison even considered using it as a railroad route as early as 1853. In that same year, the Frémont expedition party crossed the pass but viewed the sand as too great an obstacle for a successful wagon route.

In 1866, a band of Ute attacked and killed settlers near La Veta, a small settlement thirty-five miles southeast of Medano Pass. They retreated over the pass but were captured by Kit Carson and Chief Ouray.

The route has never been developed for use by wagons or as a railroad and remains much as it has always been.

Description
This route commences at the intersection of Colorado 69 and FR 559, twenty-three miles south of Westcliffe and nine miles west of Gardener. For nearly the first seven miles, the road is 2WD as it travels

A section of the trail beside the towering sand dunes

After entering the Great Sand Dunes National Monument, the road travels beside the towering sand dunes, providing a much better view of them than that from the paved roads most visitors use. In places, the sand dunes are as close as seventy-five yards from the trail. There are a number of pull-offs, but be careful as the sand can be treacherous. It is a short walk to the creek and across to the face of the dunes.

As the road travels deeper into the monument, the sand gets progressively worse and you may need to deflate your tires to about twenty pounds. You may reinflate your tires at an air compressor station, which is open during the peak season months. At other times, or if it is not available, inquire at the Visitor Center for assistance.

Signs warn you of the most difficult section, where the sand is deep and loose and steady momentum is required to avoid getting stuck. Shortly after this, you encounter the paved road (Colorado 150) that carries most visitors to the national monument.

through the Wolf Springs Ranch.

From the intersection with FR 412, it becomes a 4WD road and begins to switchback its way toward the pass. It is narrow and rough but presents no great problem as the surface is sound. The forest service has cut numerous channels across the road to protect it from erosion.

From the summit, the scenery on the descent changes, with interesting rock formations and numerous creek crossings. These are shallow enough (twelve to eighteen inches) that they should not pose any problem for a 4WD vehicle; rather, they add some variety to the trail. Use caution if it has rained recently, as the road can become boggy.

Increasing patches of sand herald the Great Sand Dunes National Monument, one of Colorado's natural wonders. Before entering the monument, the main route is intersected by a number of side roads, along many of which the sand can be a greater obstacle than it is on this section of the main road.

Current Road Conditions
Great Sand Dunes National Park
Mosca, CO 81146
(719) 378-6300

Map References
USFS   Rio Grande NF
        San Isabel NF
USGS   Huerfano #1
        Saguache #5
        Alamosa
The Roads of Colorado, pp. 135-136
Colorado Atlas & Gazetteer, p. 81

Route Directions

▼ 0.0   At the intersection of Colorado 69 and FR 559, zero trip meter and turn onto FR 559 at sign marked National Forest

	Access, Medano Pass.
9.3 ▲	End at intersection with Colorado 69.
	GPS: N 37°50.19' W 105°18.44'

| ▼ 0.3 | SO | Cross over Muddy Creek. |
| 9.0 ▲ | SO | Cross over Muddy Creek. |

▼ 6.8	SO	Cattle guard. Enter San Isabel National Forest.
2.5 ▲	SO	Cattle guard. Leave San Isabel National Forest.
		GPS: N 37°51.66' W 105°24.09'

| ▼ 7.2 | SO | Track on left. |
| 2.1 ▲ | SO | Track on right. |

| ▼ 7.3 | SO | Track on right. |
| 2.0 ▲ | SO | Track on left. |

| ▼ 7.4 | SO | FR 412 on right to South Muddy Creek. |
| 1.9 ▲ | SO | FR 412 on left to South Muddy Creek. |

▼ 9.3	SO	Medano Pass. Track on right, then gate. Zero trip meter.
0.0 ▲	SO	Continue along trail, which is now called FR 559.
		GPS: N 37°51.37' W 105°25.91'

| ▼ 0.0 | SO | Continue along trail, which is now called FR 235. |
| 6.0 ▲ | SO | Gate, track on left, then Medano Pass. Zero trip meter. |

| ▼ 0.2 | SO | Bridge over creek. |
| 5.8 ▲ | SO | Bridge over creek. |

| ▼ 0.5 | BL | Fork in track. Remain on 235. Turn right for some attractive backcountry campsites. |
| 5.5 ▲ | BR | Fork in track. Remain on 235. Turn left for some attractive backcountry campsites. |

| ▼ 1.4 | SO | Cross through creek. |
| 4.6 ▲ | SO | Cross through creek. |

| ▼ 1.6 | SO | Cross through creek. |

THE GREAT SAND DUNES

The Great Sand Dunes cover an area roughly seven miles long by five miles wide. They rise 700 feet above the valley floor to an altitude of about 8,250 feet. In summer the surface temperature of the dunes reaches 140°F.

The sand was deposited by the Rio Grande river and its tributaries over thousands of years. The dunes are fed by the prevailing southwesterly winds that flow over the Rockies and down across the floodplain of the San Luis Valley, before rising again to cross the Sangre de Cristo Mountains. Sand blown into the air accounts for only one percent of the dunes mass. Ninety-five percent is due to the wind gradually "bouncing" the grains of sand along the valley, inching them toward the valley wall where they accumulate into giant mounds.

Medano Creek travels along the eastern edge of the dunes. Each spring, the melting snow forms into the creek and travels for about ten miles before it disappears below ground. As it flows beside the dunes, it traverses broad, sandy ground, widening to many yards and constantly changing course.

The earliest inhabitation in the area was the Clovis culture as long ago as 9000 BC. The Ute were the predominant inhabitants from the late 1500s until being relocated under the terms of the Kit Carson Treaty in 1868. The first white visitor to the area may have been Don Diego de Vargas who arrived in 1694. In 1807, Zebulon Pike first documented the dunes. John Frémont and John Gunnison followed him in 1848 and 1853, respectively.

President Hoover declared the Great Sand Dunes a national monument in 1932.

SC Trail #29: Medano Pass and Great Sand Dunes Trail

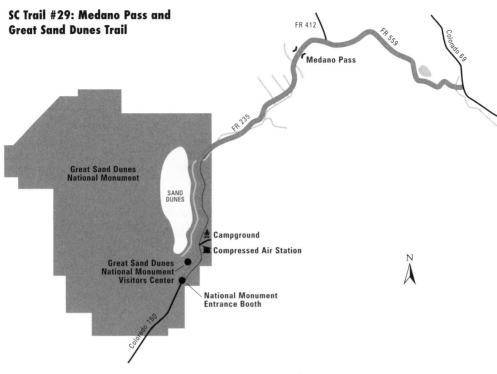

4.4 ▲   SO   Cross through creek.

▼ 1.9   SO   Track on right to cabin ruins. Then cross through creek.
4.1 ▲   SO   Cross through creek. Track on left to cabin ruins.

▼ 2.2   SO   Cluster of cabin ruins.
3.8 ▲   SO   Cluster of cabin ruins.
         GPS: N 37°49.85' W 105°26.76'

▼ 2.6   SO   Cross through creek.
3.4 ▲   SO   Cross through creek.

▼ 3.3   SO   Cross through creek.
2.7 ▲   SO   Cross through creek.

▼ 3.6   SO   Small track on right.
2.4 ▲   BR   Small track on left.

▼ 3.7   SO   Cross through creek twice.
2.3 ▲   SO   Cross through creek twice.

▼ 4.4   SO   Cross through creek.
1.6 ▲   SO   Cross through creek.

▼ 4.9   SO   Cross through creek.
1.1 ▲   SO   Cross through creek.

▼ 5.1   SO   Ruins (chimney) of old building.
0.9 ▲   SO   Ruins (chimney) of old building.
         GPS: N 37°48.47' W 105°28.99'

▼ 5.2   SO   Cross through creek.
0.8 ▲   SO   Cross through creek.

▼ 5.6   SO   Cross through large creek.
0.4 ▲   SO   Cross through large creek.

▼ 5.8-5.9 SO Tracks on left.
0.1-0.2 ▲ SO Tracks on right.

▼ 6.0   SO   Leaving Rio Grande National Forest, entering Great Sand Dunes National Monument. Zero trip meter.
0.0 ▲   SO   Cross through gate and proceed along FR 235.
         GPS: N 37°48.10' W 105°29.85'

▼ 0.0   SO   Cross through gate and proceed along FR 235.
4.8 ▲   SO   Leaving Great Sand Dunes National,

entering Rio Grande National Forest. Zero trip meter.

▼ 0.1   SO   Sand Creek trail on right. Little Medano trail on left.

4.7 ▲   SO   Little Medano trail on right. Sand Creek trail on left.

▼ 0.6   SO   Cross through creek. Then picnic area, parking, and cabins.

4.2 ▲   SO   Cabins, parking, and picnic areas. Then cross through creek.

▼ 2.4   SO   Gate and picnic spots.

2.4 ▲   SO   Picnic spots and gate.

▼ 4.8   TR   Pavement. Intersection with Colorado 150. (Note: Compressed air is available across the road.) Zero trip meter.

0.0 ▲   Proceed on Medano Pass Road (FR 235). Sign reads "Medano Pass Primitive Road."
GPS: N 37°44.66' W 105°30.39'

▼ 0.0   Proceed along Colorado 150.

1.5 ▲   TL   Opposite the National Parks building marked "private residence" and tire air station on right. Zero trip meter.

▼ 0.5   SO   Road on right to sand dunes and picnic area.

1.0 ▲   SO   Road on left to sand dunes and picnic area.

▼ 0.7   SO   Nature trail on left.

0.8 ▲   SO   Nature trail on right.

▼ 0.9   SO   Intersection. Visitor Center on the right.

0.6 ▲   SO   Visitor Center on the left. Intersection.

▼ 1.5   End at the tollbooth for Sand Dunes National Monument.

0.0 ▲   At the tollbooth for Sand Dunes National Monument, zero trip meter and proceed toward the dunes.
GPS: N 37°43.50' W 105°31.12'

Rampart Range Road

STARTING POINT   Sedalia
FINISHING POINT   Garden of the Gods in Colorado Springs
TOTAL MILEAGE   65.1 miles
UNPAVED MILEAGE   55.4 miles
DRIVING TIME   3 1/2 hours
ROUTE ELEVATION   9,370 to 5,800 feet
USUALLY OPEN   Early April to December
DIFFICULTY RATING   1
SCENIC RATING   6

Special Attractions

- Access to a network of 4WD trails.
- Easy access from Denver and Colorado Springs.
- Red rock formations and the Garden of the Gods.
- Access to numerous trail-bike and hiking trails.
- Numerous picnic spots.

Description

This is a wide, normally well-maintained, unpaved 2WD road. The road may be corrugated and suffer some erosion, but it can be safely traversed by a normal passenger car in good conditions. However, a number of more-difficult side roads make this a good spot to gain 4WD experience.

The route travels through pine forest with occasional aspen groves and past many interesting, large rock formations. Near the end of the route, the rocks turn to red as you approach the Garden of the Gods, with its 250-million-year-old sedimentary formations.

This route commences in Sedalia and heads southwest on Colorado 67 toward Deckers before turning south onto Rampart Range Road at the 9.7-mile point.

About thirteen miles after turning on to Rampart Range Road, FR 502 intersects the route on the left. This road goes to the Jackson Creek campground. It also provides an optional side road that loops back to Rampart Range Road and has sections that are more challeng-

A rock formation along Rampart Range Road

ing than the Rampart Range route; the more difficult sections would be rated 3. To take this loop, turn left off Rampart Range Road onto FR 502. Follow this road about four miles to the intersection with FR 563 (Dakan Mountain Road) (GPS coordinates are: N 39°16.91' and W 105°03.48'). Turn right onto FR 563 and head south for 1.9 miles to an intersection. Stay left and continue south reconnecting with Rampart Range Road in 5.4 miles. At this point, you will be 2.6 miles farther along Rampart Range Road than when you turned onto FR 502.

If you stayed on the main route, FR 348 intersects to the right with Rampart Range Road 0.1 miles before FR 563 enters on the left (the side-road loop discussed above). This road provides another side-road opportunity that also loops back to Rampart Range Road. To take this loop, turn right from Rampart Range Road, heading south on FR 348. At

the five-mile point, FR 351 intersects from the left (GPS coordinates: N 39°09.71' and W 105°05.01'). Turn left onto FR 351, reconnecting with Rampart Range Road in 3.7 miles, at a point 4 miles farther on than when you turned off onto FR 348.

As you approach Colorado Springs, the road starts to switchback as it descends from Rampart Range, and there are some excellent views across to the plains of eastern Colorado. The road ends at the Garden of the Gods.

If you are beginning this trail from the Garden of the Gods, finding the start of Rampart Range Road can be a little tricky. From I-25 take exit 146 and zero your trip meter. Proceed west on Garden of the Gods Road. After 2.2 miles, turn left onto 30th Street following the sign to Garden of the Gods. At the 3.5-mile point, the Garden of the Gods Visitor Center is on the left and at the 3.6-mile point turn right into the Garden of the Gods park. At the 4.1-mile point turn right onto Juniper Way Loop. There are three intersections along this road before you reach Rampart Range Road. At the intersection at 5.0 miles, bear right; at 5.7 miles, bear right; and at 5.9 miles, bear left. At the 6.2-mile point, turn right on to Rampart Range Road. This is where the trail starts.

Current Road Conditions
Pike National Forest
Pikes Peak Ranger District
601 South Weber Street
Colorado Springs, CO 80903
(719) 636-1602

Map References
USFS   Pike NF
USGS   Douglas #1
       Douglas #2
       El Paso #1
Trails Illustrated, #135, #137
The Roads of Colorado, pp. 72-73, 88-89
Colorado Atlas & Gazetteer, pp. 50, 62

Rampart Range Road about 1925

Route Directions

▼ 0.0   In Sedalia, at the intersection of US 85 (Santa Fe) and Colorado 67, zero trip meter and proceed southwest toward Deckers.

9.7 ▲   End at intersection with US 85 in Sedalia.
        GPS: N 39°26.34′ W 104°57.68′

▼ 9.7   TL Onto Rampart Range Road (FR 300). There are various information boards at the entrance. Zero trip meter.

0.0 ▲   Continue on Colorado 67 toward Sedalia.
        GPS: N 39°22.67′ W 105°05.60′

▼ 0.0   Continue along Rampart Range Road toward Devil's Head.

8.7 ▲   TR Onto Colorado 67. Zero trip meter.

▼ 0.1   SO Seasonal gate.

8.6 ▲   SO Seasonal gate.

▼ 4.5   SO USFS Flat Rocks Campground on right.

4.2 ▲   SO USFS Flat Rocks Campground on left.

▼ 4.6   SO Flat Rocks scenic overlook on left.

4.1 ▲   SO Flat Rocks scenic overlook on right.

▼ 6.2   SO FR 507 on left toward Jackson Creek Road. Telephone box.

2.5 ▲   SO FR 507 on right toward Jackson Creek Road. Telephone box.
        GPS: N 39°18.23′ W 105°05.26′

▼ 6.9   SO FR 681 forks off to the left.

1.8 ▲   SO FR 681 forks off to the right.

▼ 8.3   SO USFS Cabin Ridge picnic ground turnoff on right (0.2 miles in from FR 300).

0.4 ▲   SO USFS Cabin Ridge picnic ground turnoff on left.
        GPS: N 39°16.77′ W 105°06.30′

SC Trail #30: Rampart Range Road

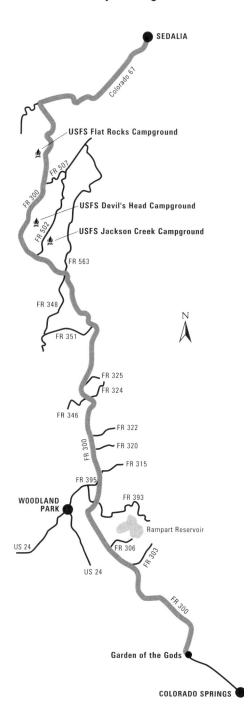

▼ 8.7   BR   Intersection: Devil's Head Campground straight ahead (0.5 miles in from FR 300). Zero trip meter.

0.0 ▲   Continue on Rampart Range Road.
GPS: N 39°16.54' W 105°06.43'

▼ 0.0   Continue on Rampart Range Road.

22.4 ▲   BL   Intersection: Devil's Head Campground on right. Zero trip meter.

▼ 2.0   SO   USFS Topaz Point picnic area on right.

20.4 ▲   SO   USFS Topaz Point picnic area on left.

▼ 4.6   SO   FR 502 on left to Jackson Creek Campground.

17.8 ▲   SO   FR 502 on right to Jackson Creek Campground.
GPS: N 39°14.01' W 105°05.73'

▼ 7.1   SO   FR 348 to Fern Creek, Colorado 67, Woodland Park, Colorado Springs on right.

15.3 ▲   SO   FR 348 to Fern Creek, Colorado 67, Woodland Park, Colorado Springs on left.
GPS: N 39°13.15' W 105°03.85'

▼ 7.2   SO   FR 563 to Dakan Mountain on left.

15.2 ▲   SO   FR 563 to Dakan Mountain on right.
GPS: N 39°13.19' W 105°03.68'

▼ 11.8   SO   Gate. Track on right goes to radio towers.

10.6 ▲   SO   Track on left goes to radio towers. Gate.

▼ 12.1   SO   FR 351 (Fern Creek Road) on right. FR 327 on left.

10.3 ▲   SO   FR 327 on right. FR 351 (Fern Creek Road) on left.
GPS: N 39°10.40' W 105°01.50'

▼ 16.7   SO   Saylor Park. FR 325 on left.

5.7 ▲   SO   Saylor Park. FR 325 on right.
GPS: N 39°06.97' W 105°02.04'

▼ 18.1   SO   FR 346 (Hotel Gulch Road) on right toward Mt. Deception.

4.3 ▲   SO   FR 346 (Hotel Gulch Road) on left.

▼ 18.4   SO   FR 324 (Ice Cave Creek Road) on left.

4.0 ▲   SO   FR 324 (Ice Cave Creek Road) on right.

▼ 19.0   SO   FR 323 (Winding Stairs Road) on left.

3.4 ▲   SO   FR 323 (Winding Stairs Road) on right.

▼ 21.4   SO   FR 322 (Balanced Rock Road) on left.

1.0 ▲   SO   FR 322 (Balanced Rock Road) on right.

▼ 22.4   BR   FR 320 (Mt. Herman Road) on left goes to Monument. Zero trip meter.

0.0 ▲   Continue on FR 300.

GPS: N 39°03.36' W 105°01.06'

▼ 0.0   Continue on FR 300.

18.7 ▲   BL   FR 320 (Mt. Herman Road) on right goes to Monument. Zero trip meter.

▼ 1.9   SO   FR 315 (Beaver Creek Road) on left (rejoins FR 320).

16.8 ▲   SO   FR 315 (Beaver Creek Road) on right (rejoins FR 320).

▼ 2.3   SO   FR 312 (Ensign Gulch Road) to Carrol Lakes on left.

16.4 ▲   SO   FR 312 (Ensign Gulch Road) to Carrol Lakes on right.

▼ 2.5   BL   Intersection with FR 393 toward Woodland Park on right. Proceed toward Rampart Reservoir.

16.2 ▲   BR   Intersection with FR 393 toward Woodland Park on left.

GPS: N 39°01.48' W 105°00.70'

▼ 3.8   SO   Leaving National Forest sign.

14.9 ▲   SO   Entering Pike National Forest.

▼ 4.0   SO   Stop sign. Intersection with Shubarth Road to the left. Woodland Park and Loy Gulch to the right. Follow sign to Rampart Road. Sign prohibits target shooting for next 17.5 miles.

14.7 ▲   SO   Intersection with Shubarth Road to the right. Woodland Park and Loy Gulch to the left.

▼ 4.8   SO   USFS Springdale Campground on left.

13.9 ▲   SO   USFS Springdale Campground on right.

▼ 6.4   SO   Rainbow Gulch Trailhead (to reservoir area) on left.

12.3 ▲   SO   Rainbow Gulch Trailhead (to reservoir area) on right.

▼ 7.8   SO   FR 306 on left to Rampart Reservoir.

10.9 ▲   SO   FR 306 on right to Rampart Reservoir.

GPS: N 38°57.70' W 104°59.72'

▼ 9.9   BR   FR 303 (Northfield Road) on left.

8.8 ▲   SO   FR 303 (Northfield Road) on right.

▼ 12.9   SO   Ridge Crest Scenic Overlook on right.

5.8 ▲   SO   Ridge Crest Scenic Overlook on left.

▼ 18.7   SO   USFS Rampart Shooting Range on right. Zero trip meter.

0.0 ▲   Proceed on Rampart Range Road.

GPS: N 38°53.86' W 104°54.68'

▼ 0.0   Proceed on Rampart Range Road.

5.6 ▲   SO   USFS Rampart Shooting Range on left. Zero trip meter.

▼ 4.1   SO   Track on right.

1.5 ▲   SO   Track on left.

▼ 5.3   SO   Rock formations—part of Garden of the Gods.

0.1 ▲   SO   Rock formations—part of Garden of the Gods.

▼ 5.6   Intersection. End at Garden of the Gods.

0.0 ▲   At Garden of the Gods, exit onto Rampart Range Road (FR 300) and zero trip meter.

GPS: N 38°51.97' W 104°53.79'

Selected Further Reading

Abbott, Carl, Stephen J. Leonard, and David McComb. *Colorado: A History of the Centennial State*. Niwot, Colo.: University Press of Colorado, 1994.

Aldrich, John K. *Ghosts of Chaffee County*. Lakewood, Colo.: Centennial Graphics, 1992.

Aldrich, John K. *Ghosts of Pitkin County*. Lakewood, Colo.: Centennial Graphics, 1992.

Bancroft, Caroline. *Colorful Colorado*. Boulder, Colo.: Johnson Books, 1987.

Bancroft, Caroline. *Unique Ghost Towns and Mountain Spots*. Boulder, Colo.: Johnson Books, 1961.

Bauer, Carolyn. *Colorado Ghost Towns— Colorado Traveler Guidebooks*. Frederick, Colo.: Renaissance House, 1987.

Beckner, Raymond M. *Along the Colorado Trail*. Pueblo, Colo.: O'Brien Printing & Stationery, 1975.

Benham, Jack. *Ouray*. Ouray, Colo.: Bear Creek Publishing, 1976.

Boyd, Leanne C. and H. Glenn Carson. *Atlas of Colorado Ghost Towns*. Vols. 1 and 2. Deming, N.M.: Carson Enterprises, Ltd., 1984.

Bright, William. *Colorado Place Names*. Boulder, Colo.: Johnson Books, 1993.

Brown, Robert L. *Colorado Ghost Towns Past & Present*. Caldwell, Idaho: Caxton Printers, Ltd., 1972.

Brown, Robert L. *Ghost Towns of the Colorado Rockies*. Caldwell, Idaho: Caxton Printers, Ltd., 1990.

Brown, Robert L. *Jeep Trails to Colorado Ghost Towns*. Caldwell, Idaho: Caxton Printers, Ltd., 1995.

Bueler, Gladys R. *Colorado's Colorful Characters*. Boulder, Colo.: Pruett Publishing, 1981.

Carver, Jack, Jerry Vondergeest, Dallas Boyd, and Tom Pade. *Land of Legend*. Denver, Colo.: Caravon Press, 1959.

Crofutt, George A. *Crofutt's Grip-Sack Guide of Colorado*. Omaha: Overland Publishing, 1885. Reprinted, Boulder, Colo.: Johnson Books, 1981.

Cromie, Alice. *A Tour Guide to the Old West*. Nashville, Tenn.: Rutledge Hill Press, 1990.

Crutchfield, James A. *It Happened in Colorado*. Helena & Billings, Mont.: Falcon Press Publishing, 1993.

Dallas, Sandra. *Colorado Ghost Towns and Mining Camps*. Norman, Okla.: University of Oklahoma Press, 1985.

DeLong, Brad. *4-Wheel Freedom*. Boulder, Colo.: Paladin Press, 1996.

Dorset, Phyllis Flanders. T*he New Eldorado: The Story of Colorado's Gold & Silver Rushes*. New York: Macmillan, 1970.

Eberhart, Perry. *Guide to the Colorado Ghost Towns and Mining Camps*. Chicago, Ill.: Swallow Press, 1995.

Fisher, Vardis, and Opal Laurel Holmes. *Gold Rushes and Mining Camps of the Early American West*. Caldwell, Idaho: Caxton Printers, Ltd., 1968.

Florin, Lambert. *Ghost Towns of the West.* New York: Promontory Press, 1993.

Foster, Mike. *Strange Genius: The Life of Ferdinand Vandeveer Hayden.* Niwot, Colo.: Roberts Rinehart Publishers, 1994.

Green, Stewart M. *Bureau of Land Management Back Country Byways.* Helena, Mont.: Falcon Press, 1995.

Gregory, Lee. *Colorado Scenic Guide: Northern Region.* Boulder, Colo.: Johnson Books, 1990.

Griffin, Wayne W. *Central Colorado 4-Wheeling Guidebook.* Aspen, Colo.: Who Press, 1994.

Heck, Larry E. *4-Wheel Drive Roads to Outback Colorado.* Aurora, Colo.: Pass Patrol, 1995.

Helmuth, Ed and Gloria. *The Passes of Colorado.* Boulder, Colo.: Pruett, 1994.

Hilton, George W. *American Narrow Gauge Railroads.* Stanford: Stanford University Press.

Jessen, Ken. *Colorado Gunsmoke: True Stories of Outlaws and Lawmen on the Colorado Frontier.* Loveland, Colo.: J. V. Publications, 1986.

Koch, Don. *The Colorado Pass Book.* Boulder, Colo.: Pruett, 1992.

McTighe, James. *Roadside History of Colorado.* Boulder, Colo.: Johnson Books, 1984.

Noel, Thomas J., Paul F. Mahoney, and Richard E. Stevens. *Historical Atlas of Colorado.* Norman, Okla.: University of Oklahoma Press, 1994.

Norton, Boyd and Barbara. *Backroads of Colorado.* Stillwater, Minn: Voyageur Press, 1995.

Ormes, Robert M. *Railroads and the Rockies.* Denver, Colo.: Sage Books, 1963.

Ormes, Robert. *Tracking Ghost Railroads in Colorado.* Colorado Springs, Colo.: Green Light Graphics, 1992.

Parker, Ben H., Jr. *Gold Panning and Placering in Colorado.* Denver, Colo.: U.S. Geological Survey, Department of Natural Resources, 1992.

Pettem, Silvia. *Colorado Mountains & Passes—Colorado Traveler Guidebooks.* Frederick, Colo.: Renaissance House, 1991.

Pettit, Jan. *Utes: The Mountain People.* Boulder, Colo.: Johnson Books, 1994.

Pritchard, Sandra F. *Men, Mining & Machines.* Dillon, Colo.: Summit County Historical Society, 1996.

Sagstetter, Beth and Bill. *The Mining Camps Speak.* Denver, Colo.: BenchMark Publishing of Colorado, 1998.

Sinnotte, Barbara. *Colorado: A Guide to the State & National Parks.* Edison, N.J.: Hunter, 1996.

Smith, Duane A. *Colorado Mining: A Photographic History.* Albuquerque, N.M.: University of New Mexico Press, 1977.

Southworth, Dave. *Colorado Mining Camps.* Wild Horse, 1997.

Southworth, Dave. *Gunfighters of the Old West.* Wild Horse, 1997.

Taylor, Colin F. *The Plains Indians.* New York: Barnes & Noble Books and Salamander Books, 1997.

Ubbelohde, Carl, Maxine Benson, and Duane A. Smith. *A Colorado History.* Boulder, Colo.: Pruett Publishing, 1995.

Waldman, Carl. *Encyclopedia of Native American Tribes.* New York: Facts on File, 1988.

Wilkins, Tivis E. *Colorado Railroads Chronological Development.* Boulder, Colo.: Pruett Publishing, 1974.

Wilson, Ray D. *Colorado Historical Tour Guide.* Carpentersville, Ill.: Crossroads Communications, 1990.

Wolle, Muriel Sibell. *The Bonanza Trail.* Chicago, Ill.: The Swallow Press, 1953.

About the Authors

Peter Massey grew up in the outback of Australia. After retiring from a career in investment banking at the age of thirty-five, he served as a director of a number of companies in the United States, the United Kingdom, and Australia. He moved to Colorado in 1993.

Jeanne Wilson was born and grew up in Washington, D.C. She lived and worked in New York City as a young adult and has been a resident of Colorado since 1993.

Traveling extensively in Australia, Europe, Asia, and Africa, the authors covered more than 80,000 miles touring throughout the United States and outback Australia in the past five years. They traveled more than 15,000 miles in Colorado to research their books.

The authors' first book, *4WD Adventures: Colorado,* is a compilation of more than 70 exciting and interesting trails in Colorado. The fully illustrated volume includes detailed information about Colorado towns, ghost towns, historical characters, wildlife, and wildflowers that relate to each route.

Photographic Credits

Unless otherwise indicated in the following list of acknowledgments (which is organized by page number), all photographs were taken by Peter Massey and are copyrighted by Adler Publishing Company, Inc., or by Peter Massey.

Page 18: Denver Public Library Western History Collection. *Page 20:* Colorado Historical Society, by William Henry Jackson. *Page 22:* Denver Public Library Western History Collection, pen sketch by Kresse. *Page 26:* Denver Public Library Western History Collection, by Muriel Sibell Wolle *Page 27:* Denver Public Library Western History Collection. *Page 34:* Denver Public Library Western History Collection. *Page 57:* Denver Public Library Western History Collection, by Charles Redmond. *Page 70:* Denver Public Library Western History Collection. *Page 74:* Denver Public Library Western History Collection. *Page 82:* Denver Public Library Western History Collection, by George E. Mellen. *Page 103:* Denver Public Library Western History Collection, by Charles Louis McClure

ORDER FORM

To purchase any of our Trails books, contact your local book or map store or order direct from Adler Publishing by any of the following methods:

Telephone orders: **800-660-5107**
Or fax your order: **310-698-0709**
Or order on-line: **4WDbooks.com**
Or mail your order to this address: **Adler Publishing Company, Inc.**
                                                  1601 Pacific Coast Highway, Suite 290
                                                  Hermosa Beach, CA 90254

- -

I understand that I may return any book for a full refund—for any reason, no questions asked.

	Price	Quantity	Total
Colorado Trails: South-Central	$16.95		
Colorado Trails: North-Central	$16.95		
4WD Trails: Southwest Colorado	$14.95		
4WD Adventures: Colorado	$29.95		

Shipping and handling $4 for the first book and $3 for each additional book. California residents add 8% sales tax and Colorado residents add 3% sales tax.

Sub Total _____

Tax _____

Shipping _____

Total _____

Send my order to:

NAME (PLEASE PRINT) _____

COMPANY _____

STREET ADDRESS _____

CITY / STATE / ZIP _____

TELEPHONE (   ) _____

Method of payment:

❏ Check or money order enclosed
❏ VISA   ❏ MasterCard   ❏ American Express

CARD NUMBER _____

EXPIRATION DATE _____

CARDHOLDER'S SIGNATURE _____